Oh,
How I Love You!

Find Freedom and Hope
In Your "Garden of Gethsemane"

Taylor Faith

Oh, How I Love You!

ISBN: 978-1-929921-24-9 (Paperback)
ISBN: 978-1-929921-26-3 (Electronic Versions)

Book design and cover concept: Thomas Taylor

Published by:

VICTORY PUBLISHERS

VICTORY
PUBLISHERS

www.Victory-Publishers.com

Oh,
How I Love You!

Dedication

I thank God that through this journey of mine, He has proven Himself to be faithful beyond what I could have imagined. Because of His unending love, I am alive and living in victory today.

Oh, how I love You, My Friend!

Taylor Faith

Table of Contents

"Faith is like radar that sees through the fog—the reality of things at a distance that the human eye cannot see."

Corrie ten Boom

Introduction

*There are battles no matter where you are in life; even
regarding your faith. I would just rather fight the battles
with Jesus than without Him.*

Everyone from the atheist to the most devout
worshipper longs to be completely and truly
loved. God has brought me through experiences
of profound helplessness and despair into victory and joy.
Ultimately, the story you're reading is about finding faith
and strength in the midst of situations and relationships
which threatened both. As you turn these pages, my
prayer is that you will discover the Father's love that is just
for you; complete, true, and ready to be poured over you.

Each chapter begins with a quote from Corrie ten
Boom, a Dutch Christian Holocaust survivor who helped
many Jews escape the Nazis during World War II. In the
first few months of my newfound faith, I read her book,
The Hiding Place. It opened my eyes to a God I never knew
before; a God far beyond the walls of churches; a God so
personal that our relationship with Him is as unique as
our fingerprints. Before I read *The Hiding Place*, I had no
idea that I could have an intimate friendship with God
NOW. I did not know that He could be so tangible, rather

than just a character we read about in the Bible. I discovered that God is present and active in our lives, constantly demonstrating His love for us, whether we know it or not. Even today, I find it impossible to fathom the depth of God's love for us. The Father waits for us to *respond* to His love, as if asking silently, "Can the cross of Christ be enough?"

Jesus says, *"Behold, I stand at the door and knock; if anyone hears My voice and opens the door, I will come in to him and will dine with him, and he with Me"* (Revelation 3:20).

I hope that reading this book is as healing for you as it was for me to write it. I pray that you come to know a bigger God than you can imagine. No matter what you have been through, or may be going through today, He has a plan for your victory; you need only to receive it!

I pray that looking at what God brought me through gives you hope and faith that everything happens for a reason, no matter how painful the experiences may be. You may not understand the reasons for your life's circumstances today, but I'm living proof that seeking God's face and presence brings victory.

So get ready! Jump up into your Heavenly Father's lap and discover just how much He loves you! I promise that the discovery makes everything worth it.

"There is no pit so deep that He is not deeper still."

Corrie ten Boom

1

The Pit

O LORD my God,
I cried to You for help, and You healed me.
O LORD, You have brought up my soul from Sheol;
You have kept me alive,
that I would not go down to the pit.

(Psalm 30:2-3)

In a dark place full of chaos and corruption, I met my Friend. At sixteen years old, my mother decided to take me out of public school. I didn't think it was fair, but little seemed fair about life at that age. Somehow I knew it was the right decision. I had been drawn into the wrong crowd and I was going nowhere fast. I *wanted* a fresh start, but I needed help. I couldn't do it on my own, but I had no idea where to look, or how to begin?

Alamogordo, New Mexico, was a small town, without much to offer. By my junior year in high school, while most of my classmates envisioned a bright future in college and beyond, all I cared about was getting my next "fix." I really wanted to be "good," whatever that meant. I longed for it, but the pit I had dug over the years was too deep for me to climb out of by myself. I longed for my family to be like the ones you might see throwing Frisbees around in the parks on Sunday afternoons. We weren't like that, however, and my reality seemed darker and more inescapable every day.

≈≈≈≈≈≈

Mom and Dad came home from work in the early evening, long after I got home from school. My mother was the first to arrive, but my little brother took most of her attention. When Dad came home later, the last thing I wanted to talk about was school. My grades were failing and nothing else seemed to matter to him. I hated sitting across from Dad at the table, seeing his disappointed expression. Neither he nor my mother seemed to care about what was *really* going on with me.

I don't know which was worse: coming home, where I was nearly invisible, or going to school, where I couldn't disappear enough. Hate and bitterness started to manifest, as tension accumulated. I wanted someone with whom I could feel safe and I resented my parents for not being able to fill the void in my heart. Years later, I learned that the void I felt was designed to be filled only by God Himself.

I hated my reality. As a little girl, I came home to an empty house. There was no one to talk to about the torment at school. The teachers knew, but they never reported it. My dad loved me the only way he knew how: he provided for the family, making sure that we were taken care of financially. There were some moments that felt like love, but they were brief and I was starved for Dad's affection and approval. The only time I really got his attention was when discipline was needed. After a while, I saw him only as someone who was married to my mother. Mom was only a little more emotionally available than Dad.

When I needed to get away, "Faraway" was a secret place in my mind where there were no bullies to remind me of how ugly and worthless I was. In Faraway, I was welcomed with open arms, and I could be whoever and whatever I chose. I was beautiful and accepted; everyone loved me; my parents were proud of me; my home was full of life and joy. Outside my land of Faraway, my parents and teachers labeled me "A.D.D." (Attention Deficit Disorder), but I didn't care. Faraway was full of happiness and peace, where grass was greener and trees were taller and fuller.

Faraway kept me from having to face what was really happening around me. It felt good to numb it all out, and to unload the weight I carried. In Faraway, nothing bothered me. It became more than just a childish fantasy; it was my alternate reality, part of a numbing routine that became my escape...however temporary. As I grew older, Faraway seemed to be less accessible and the weight of my pain became too heavy for me to carry. I used anything—including drugs and other ways of acting out—to numb the pain.

≈≈≈≈≈≈

Mom looked for a private school in the area that would take a complete loser like me. No luck. No school would accept me. Then a close friend of hers recommended a Christian boarding school for "troubled" girls, hidden in the desert mountains, about a three-hour drive away. The school promised a place of peace for those who made it their home. My mother liked the fact that it was a Christian school with strong morals and high standards. It sounded promising.

Mom arranged a phone interview with the principal to start the process. In the days went before the interview, I wondered what she would ask me. I had nothing with which to impress her. My mother probably warned her ahead of time that I was a burden. Mom was right, I was a burden. I felt empty inside, with no purpose; nothing to live for and I did whatever it took to avoid my all too sober reality.

The day of the telephone interview came and went. I spoke with the principle, Mrs. Hornell, but I have no memory of what she asked me or what I said. She must have told me what would be expected of me, and she probably described the details of private school life. As always, however, my mind wandered into the land of Faraway. A lovely vision danced in my mind of a huge gothic stone cathedral with a big red door, and me lighting candles in my little nun gown.

The interview must have gone well, because within a few days, my mother told me that I had been accepted. I felt relieved and shocked at the same time. I had one week to get everything ready. We had a lot to do: shopping for long dresses that were required for the new school; last minute medical checkups and copying health records. I found myself feeling excited! I was on my way down the right path, doing the right thing!

The week leading up to the big day for me to leave dragged on. As the days and hours ticked by, I became increasingly anxious and fearful. I didn't know when or if

I would be back. I changed my mind about going more times than I can count.

The program would last two years, and students—all "troubled" girls like me—were allowed only one 10-minute phone call each week. It seemed like a monumental change. I was sad, but everything was set and there was no question that I had to go. I had messed up things so badly with my family that living at home was no longer workable—for them or me. Seeing my mother worry and knowing I was one of the main reasons that she and Dad argued made the idea of leaving home for a Christian boarding school somewhat easier to swallow. My family needed a new beginning as much as I did.

Snow and unusually cold weather met us on the day we made the drive up the mountains to the new school. The big white icy blanket covered all signs of the coming spring, and I felt as cold as the weather. No one talked during the drive. The only sound was the low hum of the heater kicking on and wrapping itself around each of us like a blanket. My mother's soft brown eyes hung heavy from a sleepless night, while my dad's eyes were focused and steady.

I felt increasingly anxious as we neared our destination. Would I be an outcast, like I was at my previous school? I wanted to jump out of the moving car and make a run for it. I was good at running, but the desire in my heart to do the right thing for myself and my future overruled the impulse.

I don't know how long I slept, but when I awoke we were in the middle of nowhere. I had never seen a place so remote; it was a wilderness, a wasteland, and yet it was beautiful.

"We're just about there. It should be coming up shortly," my mother said. Miles seemed to separate the homes that appeared on the horizons. Evergreen trees were everywhere, so thick that it was hard to see much beyond them. It looked like Christmas—almost magical—with everything dressed in white.

Less than 20 minutes later, as the car climbed a snowy hill, I could see what would be my home for the next two years. It was completely different from what I imagined. There was no gothic church with a big red door and no nuns running around. I saw only a few country homes scattered in every direction.

"This is what the past is for! Every experience God gives us, every person He puts in our lives is the perfect preparation for the future that only He can see."

Corrie ten Boom

2

Perfect Preparation

Trust in the LORD with all your heart
And do not lean on your own understanding.
In all your ways acknowledge Him,
And He will make your paths straight.

(Proverbs 3:5-6)

A few welcoming faces appeared out of a small building, as we drove up the narrow gravel road. "Where am I? What is this place?" I thought. I couldn't shake the dreadful, sick feeling, beyond nervousness or anxiety that came over me as soon as we pulled into the gravel driveway. I *wanted* to trust that my parents knew what they were doing, and that these people, whoever they were, would help me. My insides were churning. I wanted so much to give this "starting over deal" a chance. Even though I had come to think of myself as a worthless human being, somehow I knew it wasn't too late to change and become someone worthwhile. I didn't know exactly what that looked like, but I was willing to do whatever it took to achieve it.

≈≈≈≈≈≈

A small office building was located in front of a brick cottage. Before I had time to think and get my bearings in this strange new setting, a beautiful woman came out to greet us. She was "shiny," from her silver hair all the way down to her glistening black shoes.

"Welcome!" she smiled. "I'm Mrs. Hornell. I'm the principal and pastor here." Light seemed to radiate from her face as she spoke. She escorted us into the office, where I felt soothed by the heat. The pine and cinnamon candles smelled just like my grandma's house. Mrs. Hornell began talking about when the school was opened. She said that many years ago, God had given her and her husband a heart to build the school, and everything had been accomplished through generous donations from local churches. She also shared that God had given her a heart for troubled girls. She said that only the power of Jesus Christ could heal and change a broken life.

After Mrs. Hornell's introduction to the school and ministry, she outlined what was expected of me and gave us a glimpse of what was ahead. There were chores to complete every morning, followed by school and church. Everything was mandatory. I thought, "Wow! I had no idea it was going to be like this!" I certainly had not realized that the school was going to be so serious about religion!

≈≈≈≈≈≈

The only thing I knew about this "Jesus character" that Mrs. Hornell talked about was what I learned at Bible camp when I was 12: if you didn't do what He said, brimstone and hell fire awaited you. It scared me into praying the "sinner's prayer" so that I could have my "heavenly ticket." I also prayed for the school bully to leave me alone, but it only got worse. I thought God was probably too busy saving the world to answer any of my prayers. I decided that my ticket to heaven was as lost as I was.

After years of torment, being constantly reminded of how worthless I was, eventually I believed it. I did whatever I could to escape, but my efforts only increased the darkness; it felt like a pit inside me. I wanted to change, though, and in this new setting was apparently exactly what I needed.

I was excited about the educational part of the program that Mrs. Hornell described. I wanted to learn and eventually graduate. I knew it would make my dad proud; he was a major in the Air Force, highly regarded and respected by his peers. He was a hard worker who constantly said, "Do it right the first time and you won't have to do it again!" As annoying as it was to hear him say that all the time, I found it to be true.

I wanted to be respected, well liked, and successful like my father. I wanted to hear him say that he was proud of me. I also wanted my mother to stop crying. I knew she cried a lot because of me and I wanted to see her happy and proud of me.

≈≈≈≈≈≈

After the papers were signed in Mrs. Hornell's office, we took a tour of the property. The ministry owned several acres of land, so there was plenty of walking to do. The red brick cottage nearest the office was appointed like a normal house, but with multiple bunk beds for the girls. A second cottage for another group of girls was a few hundred yards down the road. Four other cottages were on the property for off-duty staff. The program seemed to be run like a family, with 10 girls enrolled and one live-in staff member for each group of five girls in the cottages. I had many questions, but I was too timid to ask, and I tried my best to listen to Mrs. Hornell's stories.

The white school building was long enough to hold church services plus a large classroom. The walkway leading up to the massive building was a pathway bordered by rocks that were carefully placed in perfect alignment. I felt nervous as we walked into the classroom, knowing I was about to meet the people I would live with for at least the next two years. I was relieved to be greeted by a room full of smiling faces; a welcome change from my public school classrooms.

There were long rows of small wooden cubicles that separated the students from one another. At the end of the room was a teacher's desk. On the other end of the room was a chapel with an altar, a pulpit, pews, and an oak piano hidden in the corner. The combination classroom and chapel was a wonderfully efficient use of space, unlike anything I had seen before.

On the inside I was freaking out. It was all becoming so real. I didn't want to believe that this combination ministry center and boarding school for troubled girls was now my home, but it was! I wanted to trust Mrs. Hornell and her staff. I felt desperate to do whatever it took to make the situation work.

At the end of the tour, I said a quick goodbye to my parents. I couldn't look them in the eyes; I didn't want to see if they were happy or sad. It wasn't that I didn't *want* to say goodbye; I just didn't know *how* to say it. I knew that once they left, they could be a family and have their own lives more easily in my absence than in my presence.

≈≈≈≈≈≈

After my parents left, I was formally introduced to each of the students and the two teachers, who were also our live-in guardians. This new environment was going to take some time getting used to, but I knew I could manage. I was used to quick changes. Having a father in the military required our family to move every few years. Change was normal. I would just need a little time.

I was given my own Bible to read and study daily. It was torn and it looked like it had been used before...a lot. I didn't care about its appearance, but I wondered who else had searched for answers poured in its pages.

Rachel, one of the students, introduced herself as my "helper" for the next month or so. Helpers were assigned to new girls in the program to acquaint them with the daily routines, train them to fulfill their duties, and to help them learn everything that was expected in the program.

Rachel walked with me *everywhere*—even to the bathroom, where she waited outside until I opened the door. I told myself that this was the way things had to be, since all anyone knew about me was that I was as troubled as everyone else in the program. I knew that having Rachel as my "shadow" was something I had to deal with, if only for a few weeks, until I could be trusted on my own. I hoped the time would go by fast.

Devotions were held every morning and every afternoon in our cottage living room. I loved hearing about and reading how a man named Jesus healed everyone, and how His story began. I knew the story of Jesus' birth, but nothing more. I loved the book of John, because it was simple to understand.

> *In the beginning was the Word, and the Word was with God, and the Word was God. He was in the beginning with God. All things came into being through Him, and apart from Him nothing came into being that has come into being. In Him was life, and the life was the Light of men. The Light shines in the darkness, and the darkness did not comprehend it.* (John 1:1-5)

At the end of devotions, the girls spread throughout the big living room and talked to Jesus privately, as if He were present. Rachel said it was important to pray—to talk to Him—because that was how we could get to know Jesus and develop a personal relationship with Him.

When Rachel talked to Jesus, she looked giddy and serious at the same time.

I remembered when my mother tucked me in at bedtime and said prayers with me when I was small. Besides that, and the little I learned about him at Bible camp, nothing about Jesus stood out in my mind. I always believed in Him, but I didn't think He would want to spend any time with me, not out of self-pity; I truly thought He was unreachable.

≈≈≈≈≈≈

Rachel had been in the program for three years and she knew everything that was expected. The "helper system" had been implemented because there was so much assigned for each girl to accomplish in a single day; much more than I could do on my own at first. In the morning, there were Bible devotions, followed by breakfast, and then chores. Then we all got ready for school as if it were a hugely important event. Most mornings we had a short worship service in the chapel before we began our schoolwork. After school, we had a gym class, then more chores, followed by more Bible devotions. At last, bedtime would arrive. My first few days were a blur. It was hard and I can't say I did everything with the best attitude, but I tried.

I watched everyone closely, especially the staff members who were in charge of the students. I tried to understand how Jesus and the people around me were connected. If the Jesus they talked about was as great as they said, I wanted to see it for myself. I was not convinced by the students, and certainly not by the staff.

Ms. Scareton, one of the teachers and live-in guardians, supervised my group of girls. She was interesting to watch, but she made me nervous because she seemed to be irritated most of the time. She had at least five gold rings on each of her fingers, and long acrylic nails that she tapped on the table whenever one of us got on her nerves. I never knew exactly *what* bothered her, because her nail-tapping was so frequent. In addition, she had a habit of raising one over-plucked eyebrow if one of the girls said something she didn't like. I learned that it was best to keep my mouth shut and try to avoid her, but both were impossible.

Ms. Scareton seemed pleasant at times, but I could not shake the fear I felt when I was around her. Sometimes, when I noticed Ms. Scareton staring at me, she looked like a lioness before she decides whether to make a deer her prey. It was a look that made me feel sick to my stomach.

≈≈≈≈≈≈

Mornings were difficult. My chores had to be checked and approved by the staff. Everything had to be perfect and in its place. Before the girls from my cottage walked to the school building, we waited to walk with the girls from the other cottage. I was always last out the door.

Life in the program was tightly regimented. It took me several weeks to learn how to do things correctly the first time. I learned that details *are* important and that the discipline would help me later on in life. Mrs. Hornell said repeatedly, "In the long run, this will make you into the kind of normal functioning human being who will be fit for society." I wanted to be normal.

"The tree on the mountain takes whatever the weather brings. If it has any choice at all, it is in putting down roots as deeply as possible."

Corrie ten Boom

3

Putting Down Roots

He who trusts in his riches will fall, but the righteous will flourish like the green leaf. (Proverbs 11:28)

The girls seemed to be driven by a certain fear through the days. They wore this fear like clothes, but to me the fit was all wrong. I could not identify what the fear was, other than something was amiss. My impression was confirmed when I saw one of the staff become and verbally abusive to one of the girls over something that seemed entirely trivial to me. I began to realize that this was not the place of healing that Mrs. Hornell had described in her office when I first arrived. If she made an unspoken promise that first day, it appeared to have been quickly broken.

There is no fear in love; but perfect love casts out fear, because fear involves punishment, and the one who fears is not perfected in love. (1 John 4:18)

With my history of abuse at school, what should have sent alarm signals through me hardly fazed me. I was more preoccupied with facing the hard truth that I was not welcome at home and there was no other choice for me. Regardless of how things looked here, I would have to see it through, no matter what the price. I knew that I had problems; I wanted to resolve them, and I wanted badly to trust the people in charge to help me. I was determined to make it work without knowing what the ultimate cost would be.

I was among a group of girls who had been through many of the same challenges I had. It was somewhat comforting to know that they welcomed me and could relate to me. Still, I felt awkward, even in this environment. I bore the scars from ridicule and name calling that had plagued my childhood and young teenage years. No one in this new environment knew my true worth, including me. Little did I know that someone larger than all of them was watching everything.

≈≈≈≈≈≈

Soon after I arrived at the school, placement tests were necessary to determine the appropriate level for my studies to prepare for high school graduation. While awaiting the placement test results, Ms. Scareton gave me worksheets to help me better understand what I was reading in the Bible. The worksheets helped me address and solve problems, and confront issues in my life by using the scriptures. Ms. Scareton said that only the staff and Mrs. Hornell would read the worksheets. She assured me that I could write about anything, with total freedom to explore issues I was going through, or with which I was struggling.

I was excited to be given a different way—a new way—to learn about myself and to grow beyond my limitations and fears. For example, I always knew that something was missing in my life and I felt the need to search wherever and however I could to fill that void. I drove myself crazy. Nothing worked...nothing. I found it fascinating to learn about a merciful God, Who gave up His only Son so that I could live. I couldn't understand why *anyone*—especially God—would give up *anything* for me, let alone His own Son!

Before coming to the center, I had considered the Bible to be only a book with characters long dead and rules too hard to live by. I remembered remnants of Bible stories I learned as a child, and I took some comfort in recalling them. Now I recognized the need to embrace the knowledge and receive the help contained within the scriptures if I were serious about changing my life for the better. After all, what other choice was there?

It felt good to write about the challenges I was going through, and then to find a solution in the Bible. One afternoon, I recalled an old friend and missed the "good times" we had together. I decided to write about it in the worksheets to complete for Ms. Scareton that day. It was an important issue, because we were instructed, soon after we arrived, not to think about or talk to anyone other than the staff about anything that happened in our lives before we entered the program. When my old friend came into my mind, I knew it was not a good thing, and I wanted to be "good"!

That evening, Ms. Scareton asked to speak with me in the laundry room. I had learned by observation that the laundry room was not only for washing clothes but for "talking time," if one of the girls was in trouble. Every time Ms. Scareton or Ms. Albertson (the guardian for the girls in the other house) called one of the students into the laundry room, the girl usually came out teary eyed, with a look of fear on her face. All eyes were on me as I slowly made my way into the laundry room, not knowing what awaited me. I was scared and I wanted to run...far away.

"You know, I read your worksheet today," Ms. Scareton said, matter-of-factly. I tried to concentrate on what she was saying, and I struggled to understand her point. Ms. Scareton's facial expressions turned from a neutral appearance to one of all-out aggression. Her eyes were glassy and emotionless, like the look of a shark as it tears apart its food. I stayed quiet and simply listened; I didn't want her to think I was "talking back" or being disrespectful. I learned about being quiet from watching Ms. Scareton and Ms. Albertson reprimand other students and embarrass them in front of everyone. No matter how a girl responded, if the response was contrary to the staff's decision about her, she was accused of being disrespectful. She was reminded that she had come to the program to change her ways. Regardless of our pasts, I did not understand why our opinions and perceptions were so devalued. It looked to me like God did not care enough to help me understand why we were being treated so poorly.

"You know there is something wrong with you, don't you, Taylor?" Ms. Scareton asked flatly. She told me that I gave her and Mrs. Hornell the creeps, and she repeated that there was something wrong with me (as if I hadn't heard it the first time). Her tone was not one of concern, but cold and hateful. I felt like I had some sort of disease and everyone knew it except me. In any case, that was all Ms. Scareton said! I didn't know how to respond. Wasn't I in the program *because* something was wrong with me? Had I missed a class on how to be normal?

I was clueless. I did not understand Ms. Scareton's point, and it was not open for discussion. I thought the worksheets were supposed to help me solve problems. I couldn't help but wonder if the latest "problem" I had written about gave her and Mrs. Hornell the creeps, what would all my other problems do to them?

Trying to negotiate through this environment was hard enough, but suddenly it became almost unbearable when I was told that something was wrong with me and that I was giving people the creeps. If being honest about my sins and shortcomings was unnerving to them, whom could I trust? I was shocked, I felt like my chest was collapsing, and I struggled to breathe. I had no courage to fight or to defend myself. I believed everything that Ms. Scareton said to me in the laundry room that night. I felt my secret place, Faraway, calling me again to drown it all out and press forward.

I promised myself that I would guard my privacy about anything I was dealing with, and I would do only the requirements necessary to get by. I wanted to talk with other students about how they handled the staff and the worksheets, but friendships and even private conversations between students were forbidden. I wanted someone I could talk to; someone who would listen. That night, I lay in bed wondering what I had done to get here and what was wrong with me.

An almost sleepless night made getting up the next morning difficult. My mind was still reeling from the meeting with Ms. Scareton the night before. Her face haunted me, but the day's comforting busyness helped me to blot out the experience.

My school placement test results were due back, which meant that I could begin working in earnest toward graduation, my first *real* accomplishment! School was interesting and everyone worked at different levels of education. Some of the girls had dropped out of school before entering the program; some had never attended high school; and everyone had some catching up to do. Unlike public school classroom settings, the private school allowed us to work at our own pace. Each of us worked individually, with only three breaks during the seven to eight-hour school day. A great deal was accomplished, and I had much to complete for graduation.

I liked school. A sort of "honor system" was used. Except for our tests, which were graded by Ms. Scareton and Ms. Albertson, we graded our own work, with the answer key that was in front of the classroom. Our workbooks could be checked randomly, to make sure that we were grading correctly and to prevent cheating. I liked the feeling of building trust and integrity by being responsible to grade my own work. It was my fault that I had demonstrated no integrity and that I had earned no trust with my parents.

≈≈≈≈≈≈

We attended chapel every morning, before school. I loved it and I found it encouraging and interesting to listen to Mrs. Hornell or one of the staff speak to us—usually a message from the Bible—from the big white pulpit. It was almost like a church service, but not as long. I also enjoyed watching some of the students sing from the hymnals. It was as if they sang for God Himself. I was fascinated as they cried and lifted their hands, as if trying to touch Him. It was like witnessing their personal experiences of God...and I wanted that!

I thought that talking to Ms. Scareton about my desire to have the same experience as everyone else in chapel would persuade her that I was trying to do the right thing, and might even earn her respect. Her response to my questions and concerns was surprising. Her eyes didn't look cold, like they usually did. She told me that to have the experience I was seeking, I needed to ask Jesus into my heart and give my life over to Him. She said that I must confess all my sins, so I could be "saved."

"Wow! That's it?" I thought. The problem was that I could remember *some* of the sins I had committed against God, but not *all* of them! I asked Ms. Scareton what I should do. She had warned me what happened to sinners when they died. She said that God could not truly forgive me if I did not confess and repent of *every* sin. I didn't know what to do! I knew that remembering every sin I had committed was impossible. I thought that Jesus would help me remember if I just asked Him into my heart. So I did just that, hoping He would let this one thing slide, since I was trying my best to be good and to do the right thing.

Some of the girls said that they had a wonderful, magical experience when they asked Jesus into their hearts. I did not have that kind of experience, and I worried that God may not have heard me at all. I thought that if I worked hard and said the right things at the right time, God might hear me and would like me.

I tried to get out of the pit I made for myself, but feelings of guilt and condemnation pushed me back down. I felt discouraged and exhausted. I thought, "Well, I can't seem to get it right, so I may as well give up and bury myself deeper."

I know now that it is only through the grace and mercy of God, and the blood of Jesus Christ that we can be saved. It's not because of our works that salvation is possible and I thank God for that! The scriptures are very clear that only through Jesus' blood can we stand blameless before God.

You were not delivered by your own actions; therefore no one should boast.
(Ephesians 2:9, from the Complete Jewish Bible)

He entered the Holiest Place once and for all. And he entered not by means of the blood of goats and calves, but by means of his own blood, thus setting people free forever.
(Hebrews 9:12, from the Complete Jewish Bible)

So God, being the awesome Creator that He is, made the final sacrifice to take care of *all* sin, and everything that comes with it—guilt, shame, condemnation, striving, and all the rest—once and for all. No one was left out of the Father's mind that day, when His Son was sacrificed...NO ONE!

...and from Jesus Christ, the faithful witness, the firstborn of the dead, and the ruler of the kings of the earth To Him who loves us and released us from our sins by His blood. (Revelations 1:5)

Only through faith can we receive His precious gift. Had I understood the Apostle Paul's simple statement in my early exposure to the scriptures, I may have avoided years of heartache and self doubt.

"Therefore there is now no condemnation for those who are in Christ Jesus." (Romans 8:1)

"...joy runs deeper than despair."

Corrie ten Boom

4

Joy Runs Deeper
Than Despair

*For His anger is but for a moment, His favor is for a
lifetime; Weeping may last for the night, But a shout of
joy comes in the morning.*

(Psalm 30:5)

Our daily schedule didn't change much, unless
one of the staff got sick; then both houses of
girls combined into one. We had Bible
devotions together and a big slumber party. It was great
fun.

When Ms. Scareton was away, Ms. Albertson stayed
with all of us in the main house. The girls took turns
rotating in and out of the bathroom, and when it was my
turn, I quickly began brushing my teeth and taking my
shower. We were allowed a 10-minute shower—not a
second more—when our groups were in our separate
houses. Even less time was allowed when we were
together in one house. The hot water was usually gone by

the fourth person and that was me, so there was a lot of pressure to hurry. While I brushed my teeth, the others watched me anxiously, awaiting their turn. Out of the corner of my eye, I noticed one of the students staring at me with a look of total disgust on her face. She said she was going to tell Ms. Albertson on me, as if I had done something awful. I stood horrified, wondering what I had done. Was I taking too long? It couldn't have been more than five minutes, could it? No, I had a timer going and I had two minutes left. I kept a timer because there were a few times when I *had* taken too long, and hearing Ms. Scareton's irritated voice behind the bathroom door made me want to be certain never to go over my allotted time!

What was going on, I wondered? What did I do? Maybe the timer broke, I thought. I stood frozen in a feeling of panic. A few seconds later, the girl returned with Ms. Albertson. The look on her face was an aggressive glare of contempt. The student next to her looked satisfied and pleased. Mockery was etched in both of their faces.

≈≈≈≈≈≈

Even though I hadn't been in the program very long, I noticed that some of the girls would do almost anything to curry favor with the staff, even at the expense of other students; they seemed to pride themselves in creating drama, just to see another student get raked over the coals. It didn't make any difference to the staff; to them, we were former drug dealers and prostitutes with something to hide and protect.

≈≈≈≈≈≈

Finally Ms. Albertson said, "Amy told me how you were trying to gross her out while you were brushing your teeth, Taylor."

I didn't know what to say. I was in shock. Finally, I said, "I don't understand."

"You know exactly what you did," Ms. Albertson said. "Don't lie to me." Once a staff member made up her mind, that was it; she didn't need or want the facts. There was no room for talk; it was considered disrespectful. The staff and some of the girls seemed to enjoy the process of seeing someone abused in some way.

I know now that had the staff been filled with the Holy Spirit, their behavior would have been entirely different, and issues would have been brought into the light and dealt with properly. Isn't that the difference, after all, between the world and the children of God?

Ms. Albertson left after warning me never to do anything like *that* again (whatever it was). I was left with the impression that nothing I did would ever be good enough to satisfy the people in charge. I seemed to be under a kind of microscope, which the staff looked through to find anything to pick on, no matter how small, and an almost constant paranoia began to develop about what might happen next. I resigned myself to the way things were, in an undercurrent of fear and condemnation, and tried not to feel sorry for myself.

I wasn't sure how I would sleep that night after my confrontation with Ms. Albertson. The thought of being in chapel the next morning, with the music playing all around me, made peace come a little easier.

All 10 girls filed into the chapel for our service the next morning. My heart felt heavy and I wanted to run far away. I stood at my seat in the chapel, watching everyone sing in unison from the old song book and lift their hands to Jesus. Maybe they were trying to touch Him, I thought. Maybe if I raised my hands, *I* could touch Him too. Since God was so high, I might be able to reach Him if I stood up on the tips of my toes. While the others sang, I stretched as hard as I could to feel *something*. I stretched and waited, stretched and waited, and stretched some more. I so wanted something real, *someone* real—someone to love me. I struggled because I didn't even know how to love myself. I just wanted Him to be real.

All of a sudden, with my eyes squeezed shut, I saw two hands reaching down from a crown-molded ledge, trying to pull me up. It was as if I was being invited into the entrance to heaven. "It's Jesus, I know it!" I thought. I had never felt or seen the presence of God before. Was it smoke or steam pouring over the ledge? I didn't care exactly what it was that made everything so smoky; I just wanted to get a firm grip on the hands that reached down for me. My mind and heart were at war. It was hard to convince myself that this was *really* real and *truly* Him—God touching me and me touching Him.

I would have stood up on the pew to get closer, but I was afraid that I would get in trouble. I didn't want to ruin this moment...*our* moment! As I felt Him reach down, a sensation of pure warmth covered me. Time could have stopped. It was just Him and me, and it was completely quiet—no music, no voices—just His presence over and around me like a heavy blanket. I could really touch Him! He was letting me touch Him! I didn't want Him to leave or for this moment to end. I felt panic at the thought that it would soon be over and I would have to go back to school.

"Please don't leave me," I cried, "PLEASE... PLEASE! I'll fall if You leave. Please, I need You. I don't know what to do!" Soon, I began to feel that touching His fingers and His hands was not enough. I cried out again, "Please hold me! Please don't leave!" I didn't know what else to say. It was so real! I couldn't be imagining this! Why would someone so holy, touch someone like me? I was weird; I was dirty and something was wrong with me! The hands that touched mine and the warmth of truly unfiltered love that penetrated every square inch of my body were more real to me than words can describe.

Suddenly, it felt like warm oil was poured over my head and down into my face. My eyes flew open, expecting to see someone, or something, but all I found was an empty chapel. I left in a daze. I entered the classroom and made my way to my desk, in awe of what had happened. My mind and heart were still at odds over the encounter in the chapel, but I could not deny it. I also could not reconcile the real world with the one I had just left, in the presence of God.

Not even the strongest drug brought on the kind of experience I had in the chapel that morning. It was tangible; it was real and I felt loved for the first time...loved completely! Sinner or not, this was bigger than I could have ever imagined, because the love I felt was all for me!

The afternoon flew by. I was in such a state of awe from my experience that morning that I found it almost impossible to concentrate on the work in front of me. I couldn't get the experience in the chapel out of my head. I wanted *more* of the warm oil I felt being poured over my head, and His hands touching mine. I wanted to be near Him, and I wanted to hear Him the way others seemed to hear Him. I was eager to get back into prayer again, where the warmth of His presence surrounded me. How would I ever explain taking a trip to heaven, because that's exactly what it felt like?

When the afternoon chores had been checked by the staff, it was time for prayer and devotions. This was the only time during the day that was not restrained. I loved the moments in the living room, where each of us found a comfy spot to talk to God. I looked forward to that time with Jesus, when no one else existed and time was free. I found a spot for our "secret meetings" next to an old, rusty tape player that, surprisingly, still played beautiful music. I hoped that the music would drown out my voice, so that no else could listen in on my conversation with the Lord.

I found that I had little to say to Jesus. It was natural for me to be quiet with anyone I was getting to know—even Him. I tried listening to what the other girls prayed. Perhaps, I could get a clue about what Jesus wanted to hear from me. I hoped that I would see His hands again. I kept remembering what we had shared that morning in the chapel. It was a very different experience from what I had expected and how I had perceived Him in this place.

I began praying the way Rachel had taught me when I first arrived at the program. It felt intrusive—almost rude—to ask God for things or to do things for me. It felt like sending a Christmas list to Santa Claus; it was all about me, me, me. I just wanted to get to *know* Him; to know what pleased and displeased Him beyond what I found in His Book. A new kind of warmth flowed over me and enveloped me as I lay in a fetal position. I had never felt loved like this before and I never wanted it to stop. From that day on, I knew that Jesus was real. He had shown me His love for me tangibly. Most importantly, I knew who He was to me—my Friend.

≈≈≈≈≈≈

I was pretending in a pretend world, but I was aware that Jesus knew me better than I knew myself. Every word that came out of my mouth, He knew before it was even formed on my tongue. I hoped that He understood why I played the games that helped me to avoid trouble. I learned them from watching the other girls act like robots around the staff; what to say, how to say it, and don't forget...the *SMILE*. I believed that Jesus accepted me and that in devotion time at the end of the day, I could climb into His lap and everything would be okay.

I still wondered who Jesus was really. Was He like the staff here, who pretended to be nice until the "welcome" had worn off and their true characters were revealed? Would He bring up my past when I failed and rub my face in it in front of everyone? Was this what God wanted for my life? I couldn't help but think that it wasn't His highest and best purpose to live like we did in the program, but there was no one to back me up or help me through.

As far as the East is from the West, So far has He removed our transgressions from us. (Psalms 103:12)

Not only did I feel that almost everything I did was not quite good enough, but I always felt as if my past followed me around like a black cloud. When would I be truly forgiven? When a girl was in trouble for any reason, not only did the staff give them a cold shoulder, but many of the girls followed the staff's example. Was this the "peace" that Mrs. Hornell had promised when I first arrived? Was this how peace is supposed to feel?

> *A tranquil heart is life to the body, but passion is rottenness to the bones.* (Proverbs 14:30)

≈≈≈≈≈≈

The following morning, we learned that another woman, Ms. Sundry, would be joining the staff. When the announcement was made, I felt anxious and I wanted to run. The two staff we had were hard enough to handle! I wondered if I would feel nauseated around Ms. Sundry, like I felt around Ms. Albertson and Ms. Scareton.

I often thought about my options of where to live other than at the center. The only other probable home was in jail. I thought that at least the people in jail would be who they pretended to be and if not, it would not be a great disappointment. I felt guilty about these thoughts because Jesus already knew them. I wanted to be grateful for the second chance He had given me.

≈≈≈≈≈≈

The staff had very creative ways of keeping us very busy, and I liked that. One of my projects was to read *The Hiding Place*, by Corrie Ten Boom. I couldn't help but compare Ms. Scareton and Ms. Albertson to the Nazi soldiers I read about in the book. Even though our bones were not being broken and our bodies were not being burned alive, it felt as if our minds were being tortured and spirits were being killed.

I actually thought I *deserved* the treatment I received, and that this was God's doing. I thought I must have needed to be punished. I did not realize at the time that I was actually denying the CROSS of Christ! Although I believed, in some twisted way, that the staff knew best and I needed to respect them, I felt sick deep inside at their behavior toward me and the other girls. I knew I had done little in my life that was right, and that was why I was in the program. What I could not understand was why I continued to hear about a mistake I had made for a month afterward. I often thought of the scripture about how Jesus died to forgive us so that our sins would be remembered no more. Why was Jesus still on the Cross here? Did I miss something? I felt aghast at my treatment while, at the same time, I felt deserving of it all. I just wanted to learn from my mistakes and move on.

Isaiah 43:18-26 clearly addresses this:

> *Do not call to mind the former things, or ponder things of the past. Behold, I will do something new, now it will spring forth; Will you not be aware of it?*
>
> *I will even make a roadway in the wilderness, rivers in the desert. The beasts of the field will glorify Me, the jackals and the ostriches, because I have given waters in the wilderness and rivers in the desert, to give drink to My chosen people. The people whom I formed for Myself will declare My praise.*
>
> *Yet you have not called on Me, O Jacob; But you have become weary of Me, O Israel. You have not brought to Me the sheep of your burnt offerings, nor have you honored Me with your sacrifices. I have not burdened you with offerings, nor wearied you with incense.*
>
> *You have bought Me not sweet cane with money, nor have you filled Me with the fat of your sacrifices; rather you have burdened Me with your sins, you have wearied Me with your iniquities.*
>
> *I, even I, am the One who wipes out your transgressions for My own sake, and I will not remember your sins. Put Me in remembrance, let us argue our case together; state your cause, that you may be proved right. "*

"*When a train goes through a tunnel and it gets dark, you don't throw away the ticket and jump off. You sit still and trust the engineer.*"

Corrie ten Boom

5

Sitting Still

The LORD will fight for you while you keep silent.

(Exodus 14:14)

Ms. Sundry came to stay with us when I had been in the program about six months. She was much older than the other staff and there was a softness about her. I watched her closely for several days, thinking, perhaps that she may only have appeared to be nice during her first days on the job. Ms. Sundry's face looked very different from the other staff when she spoke to the students. She appeared to be truly sincere and her tone of voice lacked the harshness I had become so used to hearing from Ms. Scareton and Ms. Albertson.

During our evening prayers, Ms. Sundry stood in the middle of the room and prayed to Jesus in her spirit-filled language. It was a beautiful sound and, even though I had no idea what she was saying, somehow the language made sense. I knew that Ms. Sundry was praying for all of us. Most of the time, she went around the room and prayed for each girl.

There was much discussion among the girls about "intercessory prayer": praying for sinners. I had never seen prayer for others until Ms. Sundry arrived, but she showed us what it looked like. Sometimes she cried when she prayed, like she knew something about us or about the person for whom she was praying. It seemed that she and Jesus shared secrets and I loved to watch her pray. I even found myself feeling a little jealous, knowing that she could really hear Him. It was a blessing to see how He must have delighted in her and how she delighted in Him.

Ms. Sundry was an example of God in the flesh to me. A spirit of peace accompanied her when she was on duty. It was obvious that she loved us and wanted the best for us, even though I never heard her say it.

I wasn't personally familiar with the Holy Spirit until Ms. Sundry came. When I heard others praying in the spirit—in tongues—it sounded worked up and showy. When Ms. Sundry prayed in the spirit, the presence of God rested on her and around her. After watching her for a few weeks, I wanted what she had.

Ms. Sundry did not have the glare in her eyes that Ms. Scareton or Ms. Albertson did. She didn't embarrass the girls to assert her authority or to demonstrate her power. Her authority was quiet, but obvious. I hoped she would never leave. When she was gone for any reason, the girls irritated the other staff, because we asked them when Ms. Sundry would return. Except for Mrs. Hornell, during her infrequent visits to our cottages, Ms. Sundry was the only one on staff who went around the room and prayed for us. I thought of her as an ancient warrior, who talked to God for us; who helped us pray to overcome anything we may have been facing. She was truly my Jesus in the flesh.

Ms. Sundry was consistent and fair with everyone and, thank God, she had no favorites. The Bible clearly talks about how destructive favoritism can be:

> *My brethren, do not hold your faith in our glorious Lord Jesus Christ with an attitude of personal favoritism. For if a man comes into your assembly with a gold ring and dressed in fine clothes, and there also comes in a poor man in dirty clothes, and you pay special attention to the one who is wearing the fine clothes, and say, 'You sit here in a good place,' and you say to the poor man, 'You stand over there, or sit down by my footstool,' have you not made distinctions among yourselves, and become judges with evil motives?*

Listen, my beloved brethren: did not God choose the poor of this world to be rich in faith and heirs of the kingdom which He promised to those who love Him? But you have dishonored the poor man. Is it not the rich who oppress you and personally drag you into court? Do they not blaspheme the fair name by which you have been called?

If, however, you are fulfilling the royal law according to the Scripture, "YOU SHALL LOVE YOUR NEIGHBOR AS YOURSELF," you are doing well. But if you show partiality, you are committing sin and are convicted by the law as transgressors. For whoever keeps the whole law and yet stumbles in one point, he has become guilty of all. For He who said, "DO NOT COMMIT ADULTERY," also said, "DO NOT COMMIT MURDER." Now if you do not commit adultery, but do commit murder, you have become a transgressor of the law. So speak and so act as those who are to be judged by the law of liberty. For judgment will be merciless to one who has shown no mercy; mercy triumphs over judgment. (James 2:1-13)

I wanted to talk to Jesus the same way that Ms. Sundry did. I wanted the secret language that only Jesus and my spirit could understand. I wanted His spirit to dwell in me and for Him to be my Helper, the same way He was for

Ms. Sundry. I wanted "the consoler" to be with me, because I had to have Him to survive in the midst of my circumstances.

When I talked to Ms. Sundry about it, she said that all I had to do was ask the Lord and, when the time was right, He would give His Holy Spirit to me. I think she wanted it for me as much I did. I was surprised that Ms. Sundry didn't lose her voice, for all the praying she did for me to receive the Holy Spirit.

I wasn't sure what to expect. Would I hear a voice from heaven? Would there be a dove flying around? I knew there would be evidence, but how would I know that I wasn't just making something happen? God worked it all out, totally by surprise, during prayer and devotion time. I was repenting for something I had done that day, and after dwelling on it for several minutes, suddenly my language was not English! I still find it difficult to describe the experience. At first I thought that God was gracefully saying, "Okay, let's change the subject." It was a language that I had never heard, for which my brain had no comprehension, and in which my conscious mind was not engaged. I realized, however that my first encounter with the Holy Spirit through sounds, was the same as the experience recorded in the book of Acts, when the Holy Spirit came upon the early disciples:

When the day of Pentecost had come, they were all together in one place. And suddenly there came from heaven a noise like a violent rushing wind, and it filled the whole house where they were sitting. And there appeared to them tongues as of fire distributing themselves, and they rested on each one of them. And they were all filled with the Holy Spirit and began to speak with other tongues, as the Spirit was giving them utterance.

Now there were Jews living in Jerusalem, devout men from every nation under heaven. And when this sound occurred, the crowd came together, and were bewildered because each one of them was hearing them speak in his own language. They were amazed and astonished, saying, "Why, are not all these who are speaking Galileans? And how is it that we each hear them in our own language to which we were born? Parthians and Medes and Elamites, and residents of Mesopotamia, Judea and Cappadocia, Pontus, and the province of Asia, Phrygia, Pamphylia, Egypt, and the districts of Libya around Cyrene, and visitors from Rome, both Jews and proselytes, Cretans and Arabs — we hear them in our own tongues speaking of the mighty deeds of God."

And they all continued in amazement and great perplexity, saying to one another, "What does this mean?" But others were mocking and saying, "They are full of sweet wine." But Peter, taking his stand with the eleven, raised his voice and declared to them: "Men of Judea and all you who live in Jerusalem, let this be known to you and give heed to my words. For these men are not drunk, as you suppose, for it is only the third hour of the day; but this is what was spoken of through the prophet Joel:

"AND IT SHALL BE IN THE LAST DAYS," God says, "THAT I WILL POUR FORTH OF MY SPIRIT ON ALL MANKIND; AND YOUR SONS AND YOUR DAUGHTERS SHALL PROPHESY, AND YOUR YOUNG MEN SHALL SEE VISIONS, AND YOUR OLD MEN SHALL DREAM DREAMS; EVEN ON MY BONDSLAVES, BOTH MEN AND WOMEN, I WILL IN THOSE DAYS POUR FORTH OF MY SPIRIT,"

And they shall prophesy. (Acts 2:1-18)

Before the language of my spirit formed, my prayer times were occupied with a routine of repenting and feeling guilty. I thought that if I said, "I'm sorry," enough times and mourned sufficiently over the sins I had committed or the mistakes I had made, they were redeemable. Ms. Sundry taught me that when I didn't know what else to pray, the Holy Spirit would speak for me. I loved knowing that Jesus and I were closer; that during the most difficult times, His warmth would cover me, and the calm of His presence would heal any negative feelings.

≈≈≈≈≈≈

I noticed, over a period of weeks, that I saw less and less of Ms. Sundry. I never wanted her to leave and I wondered why she wasn't working as much, but I was not free to ask. I felt strangely guilty for enjoying the peace of her presence, in contrast to feeling paranoid and frightened around Ms. Albertson and Ms. Scareton.

Ms. Sundry left the program after only four months and whatever peace she had brought left with her. She was the closest person to the Jesus I had seen, and she looked nothing like the Jesus Who was preached at the center. It was heartbreaking to see Ms. Sundry leave; confusing and disorienting to no longer have her with us. For months I wondered why she left. Was she sick? Was she working somewhere else? I had a feeling that the answer was none of those; that she had been *asked* to leave. Two years later, I discovered that Ms. Sundry had been dismissed for *failing to discipline the girls enough*.

≈≈≈≈≈≈

I pressed into my school work and the "busyness" of each day as I struggled to block out Ms. Sundry's absence.

I used the work to numb myself to anything I didn't want to deal with. So much was overwhelming and confusing about the program and the people in charge. The work in front of me each day was all that seemed to make sense.

After being at the center for almost a year, I had caught up with much of my school work. It was a great feeling of accomplishment. Not all the girls stayed in the program through graduation. When someone quit, it motivated me to try even harder to finish what I had begun, despite the craziness surrounding me.

I was excited when the staff told me that my parents would be visiting in a few weeks. I wanted them to see all the progress I had made, both in the program itself and in my school work. My grades had improved from failing to almost straight A's! For the first time in my life, I was proud of myself. I was truly amounting to something...to *someone*!

One afternoon, Ms. Albertson pulled me aside from the other girls in the classroom to "talk about something." Even after a year in the program, the ominous sound of her words made my heart jump into my throat. I tried hard not to look at her face, but as I pulled a seat up to her desk, there was nowhere else to look. My heart felt as if it had stopped when I met her cold, mocking eyes.

"Do you have something you want to tell me?" Ms. Albertson asked. My mind went blank. My hands began to shake and sweat, as they always did when she or Ms. Scareton wanted to "talk."

"No," I said hesitantly. Even if I *did* have something to say to her, she wouldn't listen anyway. She proceeded to tell me that I had cheated on my school work. The reason she said she knew was because she had found blank pages in my workbook. I began to panic, trying to figure out how in the world I had not noticed something so obvious! I had no idea how pages could have been left blank, unless I had skipped some while correcting my work. Even so, I wondered how Ms. Albertson could have gotten my workbook without my knowing, since we kept them with us at all times. The staff periodically checked our school work, but they always asked us to see our workbooks. The staff would only glance through them to see if they looked right. I had been in the program long enough to know that every page had to be completed. If I were going to cheat, I would have filled in the blanks with *something*, so at least it would have *appeared* to have been completed. Still, somehow I had managed to skip over some questions.

The staff assumed a student had cheated if she failed the test at the end of a workbook more than once, but I hadn't failed any tests! There had to be a reason for Ms. Albertson to check my workbook without my knowledge. I could not imagine why I had been chosen for such close scrutiny on that particular day.

My heart felt heavy and I had trouble breathing. A year's worth of dammed up tears came rushing out all at once. I had learned not to cry—it was considered a "pity party" and that was forbidden—but now I couldn't help crying. I felt helpless, hopeless, and outraged at the same time; not just because I had missed whole pages of work, but because I knew that no matter how hard I tried to explain or defend myself, I would be knocked down. All I could voice through my despair and my tears was a pathetic plea, "I DIDN'T CHEAT! PLEASE BELIEVE ME! PLEASE!"

Ms. Albertson said flatly, "I've already spoken to Mrs. Hornell and she is extremely disappointed and hurt." My tears were uncontrollable to the point that my whole body shook.

"STOP IT! STOP IT!" Ms. Albertson yelled. Her voice was as uncontrollable as my sobs. "You're lying to me!" she declared. I knew that, once again, nothing I had to say would be heard.

Ms. Albertson said that Mrs. Hornell wanted to talk to me on the phone. Honestly, I just didn't care. "Keep 'em coming," I thought. "Shoot me, for all I care!" For the first time in a year, I felt a familiar numbness take over my body, as it had before I came to the program. I had learned to produce this sensation without the help of drugs and I was quite good at it. I found it easy to disconnect from my emotions once again. Some experts describe sociopaths in a similar way: "They kill and mutilate their victims, and within minutes after the killing, they go out for ice-cream..."

I *felt* nothing because in this place I *was* nothing! It was utterly heartbreaking to be in the midst of such an experience. Instead of a solution, I faced punishment.

Mrs. Hornell would normally have seen me in her office, but she was at home recovering from a black widow spider bite. Apart from the fact that, as always, nothing was up for discussion, all I remember about the phone call was that she said I had made her feel worse than her spider bite.

After Mrs. Hornell said everything she had on her mind, and I had answered, "Yes ma'am," at all the appropriate times, the phone call ended. Ms. Albertson told me that my parents had been notified about the incident and that their upcoming visit had been cancelled.

A year later, Ms. Scareton addressed something about my school work in front of the other students. I listened in horror as she said how shocked she was that the ground hadn't opened up and swallowed me whole. She said there was a special place that God had in mind for people like me (i.e., "hell").

Two years into my stay at the center, Mrs. Hornell decided to look into why my work was sometimes incomplete. Test results showed that I was dyslexic. Finally there was an answer, but it was too late to erase Ms. Scareton's words from my mind and heart.

Why didn't God intervene sooner? He knows the hearts of everyone and He is always watching, but His perspective is often very different from ours. While His timing may not seem right to us, it is always perfect.

"For My thoughts are not your thoughts, Nor are your ways My ways," declares the LORD. (Isaiah 55:8)

"The first step on the way to victory is to recognize the enemy."

Corrie ten Boom

6

The Presence
of the Enemy

*In the year of King Uzziah's death I saw the Lord
sitting on a throne, lofty and exalted, with the train of His
robe filling the temple.* (Isaiah 6:1)

After the "meltdown" with Ms. Albertson and Mrs. Hornell, I was unsure about how to approach Jesus in prayer. He knew what had happened, but I didn't know what He thought about it. I found my "secret spot" and, instead of praying, I curled up next to the old tape player and listened to the words of the song that played. It was my favorite song by Dennis Jernigan. I remember hearing the words clearly, as if someone had turned the volume up:

"How I love you, child. I love you!"

The words played over and over again. I wanted to hear Jesus sing over me the way He was singing over Dennis Jernigan. Lying there in the cottage's living room,

I closed my eyes; the voices of the girls around me grew faint, and I became quiet and peaceful. Suddenly, I found myself in a large room, almost like a hotel lobby. Golden rays of light enveloped the entire room. I couldn't move from my fetal position, but I was able to look up. There He was...my Friend!

I saw a throne-like seat, with clouds around it, at the far end of the large room. My Friend was standing in front of His throne facing east, His face like flint and holding a sword in His right hand. He looked down, concentrating on something. Still frozen, I saw what had captured my Friend's attention: dense black smoke hovered over a heated battle, the sound from which became louder by the second. I looked back and saw that my Friend appeared to be waiting for something to happen. All I could do was moan, "HOLY...HOLY... HOLY..." His love covered me completely. It was almost too heavy and I could hardly contain all of who He was inside of me. I felt protected and warm again, like someone had wrapped a massive blanket around me.

Slowly, the voices of girls praying and the music from the tape player came rolling in, as if someone had just turned up the volume of life's noises. I almost felt guilty for how it offended my senses, but it was just *so noisy* here! Even in the midst of the noise, I felt the peace return that had disappeared with Ms. Sundry. Suddenly, nothing else mattered!

≈≈≈≈≈≈

The day I feared most finally came: the weekly phone call from my parents. Even though they had been told that I "cheated" on my school work, the staff made me confess it to my parents. They insisted that I repeat back to them *exactly* what they wanted me to say to my parents, or they would interrupt the 10-minute call. On the phone, I wanted to scream, "*I didn't cheat,*" but, with the staff monitoring the call, I played a familiar, submissive role. I lied to my parents for the first time since they had brought me to the center and it broke my heart. I hated the staff, more than ever, for what they had made me do. I was building a tremendous hatred and bitterness toward them; yet, strangely, I felt an amazing sense of peace!

≈≈≈≈≈≈

My punishment for "cheating" was to arrange the rocks that bordered the path leading to the chapel. I wondered how I would ever make the path look as perfect as was expected. For example, no weeds could touch the rocks; in fact, no weeds were to be found anywhere near the path!
Even though I hated the punishment, I found myself

feeling light and joyful. I also had time to think. During our busy days, except for devotions, we never had time to ourselves to think and to be at peace. I couldn't help but wonder where God was in all of this. If Mrs. Hornell *really* knew Jesus, as she claimed, why didn't she see what was wrong with the ministry she headed? Why didn't she see how abusive and manipulative her staff was toward the girls? It was confusing and there were no answers.

After hours of clearing the ground along the path, I carefully laid the rocks end-to-end until the entire path was aligned, perfectly shaped, and bordered.

≈≈≈≈≈≈

One day, in the little free time I had, I asked God what He would have me read in His Book. I was already studying the New Testament and I felt that my knowledge of the Old Testament needed a little help. As I flipped through the pages, I stopped in the first book of Samuel. I had read a few scriptures from it before, during church on Sundays. This time, however, I read from the beginning about how everything started for Israel's second king, David. His life fascinated me, because no matter how badly he messed up, his heart was focused on God.

The LORD has sought out for Himself a man after
His own heart, and the LORD has appointed him as
ruler over His people. (1 Samuel 13:14)

I loved the way that David and the Lord loved each other. No matter what happened in David's life, whether he was running from a wicked king or toward a battle, he knew that everything was in God's hands. David so respected God that he refused to harm Saul, whom he called "God's anointed," even when Saul was after David's life. God used the misfits and malcontents in Saul's kingdom to make David into Israel's greatest king. It was refreshing to have these and other stories to look forward to, in an environment of unvaried routine.

I realized that the bullies and the name calling I had endured as a child served to mold me into someone who could empathize with and help other outcasts and rejects from their families and environments. I realized that God had blessed me with insights that could help others like me. As much as I hated to admit it, I could see that God had ordained my presence at this bizarre ministry center and private school, because here I met Jesus, my Friend.

≈≈≈≈≈≈

Keeping a positive attitude wasn't easy, but learning the "games"—how and when to smile and how to respond properly—kept me somewhat safe. I busied myself with the daily routine, because I knew I was making Jesus proud, and I was keeping the staff out of my way. I reminded myself that I was here *on purpose*; Jesus knew all the reasons why and that was all that mattered.

I struggled to grasp the concept that I was good enough for Jesus to love, because I never felt good enough for anyone else, including me. He was the only one Who could perceive and support me as God's *"new creation"* (Galatians 6:15).

≈≈≈≈≈≈

Sometimes, I would forget details of what the staff had told me to do. One day, Ms. Scareton told me to carry a clipboard and write down every instruction I was given. I thought the clipboard was a great idea! I was tired of forgetting things, getting into trouble, and being labeled as the "spacey troubled girl."

I began carrying the clipboard immediately, enthusiastically writing down everything I was told to do. Within only a few hours, Ms. Scareton said that she needed to talk to me. "Oh God," I thought, "what now?"

With her hand on her hip and one over-plucked eyebrow raised, she hissed, "You think you're so smart with your little clipboard, don't you?" Ms. Scareton was always picking at something, so I wasn't surprised that pulled me aside, but her question confused me, since she had given me direct instructions to carry the clipboard in the first place!

Asking a question would have been considered talking back, and Ms. Scareton clearly relished her position of power. One mistake on my part meant a phone call to my parents, and that scared me more than anything. Although her comment made no sense, I responded meekly, "No, ma'am, I didn't realize."

Later I thought, "Something has to be done. This isn't right and I'm tired of being quiet!" I decided to tell Mrs. Hornell privately what had happened. Even though she was rarely visible, I liked Mrs. Hornell and I wanted to make her proud. I rationalized that her years of working with the worst troubled girls may have taken a toll on her. How would she ever believe what was truly going on under her supervision unless someone intervened? At the first opportunity, I told Mrs. Hornell that Ms. Scareton was simply being mean, and that the clipboard incident was only one small example of many other hurtful situations that Ms. Scareton had instigated.

Mrs. Hornell called Ms. Scareton and me into her office. Ms. Scareton called me an *"accuser of the brethren"* (Revelation 12:10), and told me that I was ungrateful to be in the program. She twisted my words into something other than what I had intended and Mrs. Hornell believed her. After all, I was only a student, and a "troubled girl" at that. I was sentenced to a "bean fast" for a month—nothing but plain beans for every meal—and I had to clean out the rat-infested dumpsters.

Before I left Mrs. Hornell's office, she told me about a voice message from my mother, saying that she could not afford to buy new clothes for me that were only necessary because of my "lack of self control." I had gained 30 pounds while at the school and none of the clothes I had brought with me fit anymore. The few outfits I had, from donations to the center, were fine with me, but Mrs. Hornell had taken it upon herself to tell my mother about the situation as she saw it. It seemed to be a deliberate and calculated "knockout blow," delivered when I was already vulnerable. When I finally left the office, my mind was a blur. I wanted to die. I felt totally alone and isolated, like I imagined Jesus did in the garden of Gethsemane, when everyone he knew and loved left him.

Over the next several days, I began to think that Ms. Scareton and Mrs. Hornell were right about me. I convinced myself that I really *was* ungrateful. Maybe I really *was* unworthy and *did* lack self-control! Maybe Ms. Scareton and Mrs. Hornell had not acted hurtfully after all. Deep inside, however, I knew better; something was truly dark here. I learned to "bite my tongue" from that time on, and my heart became gradually less receptive to anyone's false accusations.

God came to my defense one day: I had recently moved to the other cottage a few blocks away from the other one. We were also further from the chapel and school, so we all had to get up a little earlier to meet the other girls. As we were getting ready one morning, Ms. Scareton rushed out of her dark room, yelling for us to get to the other house immediately. It had to have been an emergency because only one of her eyebrows was drawn on, and she would *never* have left the house without both of her eyebrows! Even though some of us were still in our pajamas, we all went to the other house.

"Wow! What's going on?" I thought, "Could it be a fire?" Occasionally a pipe burst from the frost, but it was never this kind of emergency. As we arrived at the other house, we were surprised to find a student in the staff room, which was absolutely forbidden. She was talking on the phone and crying hysterically. Ms. Scareton rushed in to take the phone from her. Where were Ms. Albertson and Tory (a student who had arrived two weeks before me)? We all piled into the living room, wondering what had happened and why the student was not being reprimanded for being on the phone *and* in the staff room! Mrs. Hornell pulled up in the gravel driveway a few minutes later and rushed inside the cottage. Everyone took a seat in the living room and anxiously waited for her to gather her thoughts.

"Oh my, God, she's crying!" I thought.

Finally, after a long pause, the words finally came flooding out, "Ms. Albertson and Tory have run away! Please, tell me! Did anyone see this coming?" All of us shook our heads. We were speechless.

Mrs. Hornell questioned us, one by one, to determine whether any of us had felt like running away; she called it a "running spirit." One girl raised her hand and said that she had thought about running away; slowly a couple more girls agreed. As troubled as everyone thought I was, I kept my hands down and my mouth shut. The truth was that I had wanted to run away before I had arrived, and certainly soon after that, but I had learned to keep quiet. I didn't trust Mrs. Hornell or anyone else in the program. Jesus was the only One I could trust to keep my secrets. In Him alone I was confident. After the meeting with Mrs. Hornell, we were given a contract to sign, in which we agreed never to tell anyone what had happened that morning.

≈≈≈≈≈≈

Jesus and I talked together frequently, so when I didn't hear from Him, my heart literally ached. When I couldn't feel His presence, I thought I had disappointed Him. I pursued Him and He was never quiet for too long. Jesus always found ways to comfort me, convincing me of His great love for me. Just when I felt like quitting, Jesus refreshed me with His love and favor. It was as if I had found someone that no one else knew about. Jesus was all mine; my secret; my Friend.

"*Happiness isn't something that depends on our surroundings...It's something we make inside ourselves.*"

Corrie ten Boom

7

NEW!

Jesus said to him, "No one, after putting his hand to the plow and looking back, is fit for the kingdom of God."

(Luke 9:62)

The day Ms. Albertson ran away brought a huge sense of release in my spirit. All the waiting for God to intervene on my behalf came to a climax and the meaning of the vision at the Lord's throne room became clearer. I recognized the significance of the sword in His hand and His focus on a battle raging below Him. I knew the Lord had gone to battle for me when Ms. Albertson left, and suddenly there was one less enemy to worry about. Some students were sad about Ms. Albertson's departure, and I felt a little guilty because I had to admit I hated her and I was glad she ran away. In any case, the environment was decidedly more pleasant.

Many of the bad attitudes I had when I entered the program, and had hoped to replace with others more productive and positive, had turned into unforgiveness and anger. I wondered when the cycle of hate and bitterness would end and whether I would ever be mentally and emotionally whole and healthy.

≈≈≈≈≈

Mrs. Hornell took the girls out occasionally to minister and raise funds at local churches. Telling my "testimony"—the story of everything I had done before I entered the program—was unbearably painful. It was embarrassing to watch people's expressions turn into pity and I hated feeling like a source of weird entertainment. I had come into the program to get better, but wearing the "troubled" label everywhere we went was demoralizing. I could never really leave my past behind me. When was I going to be the *"new creature"* that the Apostle Paul wrote about? Was I *always* going to be troubled? Ironically, one of the changes that occurred in the year after Ms. Albertson ran away was that I was given the "privilege" of taking the lead during most of our ministry trips to raise money for the school.

> *Therefore if anyone is in Christ, he is a new creature;*
> *the old things passed away; behold, new things have come.*
> (2 Corinthians 5:17)

On the way back to the school from one of our trips, I tried talking to Mrs. Hornell about how I felt. I really wanted some answers about why we were still called troubled and why we had to share our testimonies everywhere we went. I came here to be new and to clean up my past, rather than to have it constantly follow me around like a dark cloud.

I understood that there are times when people need to hear where we came from, to reach the lost and to minister people into victory, but why was our past *continually* brought up? Why couldn't we just be guided by the Holy Spirit? It seemed to me that if a ministry were truly ordained by the Lord, He would provide funding in different ways. Mr. and Mrs. Hornell's ministry was well known in the area, but there seemed to be a lack of faith that the Lord would provide. Bringing all this up to Mrs. Hornell was scary and it turned out to be a big mistake. The feeling that my concerns and questions would not be received was right; Mrs. Hornell reprimanded me for being prideful.

≈≈≈≈≈

I often fantasized about when I would finally leave the program and be free to become the person I knew I was called to be. I often fought with the idea that the "troubled girl" label would always be with me, but deep inside, I knew I was called beyond it. I knew that I had to keep believing in myself and in the One Who brought me here. I had to hold fast to the faith that I would overcome in the end, whatever that looked like.

God gave me amazing grace to rise above everything in my circumstances. Looking back, I wonder how I stayed there, amidst the contradictions that surrounded and affected me. My Friend Jesus told me, over and over, that He had a specific purpose for me there. His assurance became an increasingly important focus for my thoughts. Sure, I wanted to make my parents proud, but it was Jesus that I *really* wanted to make smile. No matter where I was, while asleep or in class, I felt His warmth. The end of my time was coming closer every day. I knew exactly how much work I needed to accomplish for graduation; that was my prize and my eyes were firmly fixed on it.

≈≈≈≈≈≈

I saw many girls come and go, while I was in the program. It was important for me to make my time count, for Heaven's sake and my own. God began giving me a focused mind to finish the program, to graduate, and to complete whatever He had for me to do. I owed

Him at least my full attention and commitment to finish. Sadly, although I know better today, I believed then that God would reject me if I did not complete the program.

In a strange way, I had grown to love and respect Mrs. Hornell. She had corrected me more times than I could count for disagreeing with her. She insisted that I needed to work on the issue of pridefulness, because I was being rebellious by not agreeing with her. I *wanted* to agree with her. I had been indoctrinated into the belief that she and the staff always knew best, and that I *was* the rebellious and prideful person she said I was. I repented constantly; I did whatever she asked, to please her and God.

≈≈≈≈≈≈

A new staff member was hired to fill Ms. Albertson's position until a full time replacement could be found. Ms. Marci had been a student at the program a few years earlier. The fact that she had graduated gave me hope for my own graduation, and hope that I too could amount to something.

After the first couple of weeks following Ms. Marci's arrival, her true character began emerging. The change caught me by surprise. The girls in our house all at around the huge kitchen table each morning, doing our hair and makeup. Bedrooms were too small, and since only one girl at a time was allowed in the only bathroom, the kitchen table was the one place big enough for all of us to get ready at the same time.

One morning, as Ms. Marci sat with us, preparing her face and hair, she commented on how horrible we all looked without makeup. I watched the girls' faces drop as the shock of her comment pierced our hearts. Ms. Marci laughed as she went on getting ready for the day. I knew I was no Miss America, but what made her think that her comment was helpful in any way?

Ms. Marci began teasing the girls with a degrading tone of voice. She clearly believed that nothing anyone did was good enough. She cleverly chose only a few of us to pick on at a time. She knew the power she had and how much Mrs. Hornell trusted her. I was frightened, because I knew that any cry we made would not be heard.

Ms. Marci often looked at me in the same way that Ms. Scareton did, only worse: mockery and hardness were slashed into Ms. Marci's expression. Her looks were dark, like a bully gloating over her victim; it sent chills up my spine. I felt doomed.

I wondered, since the school was a "ministry," if the authorities in churches were like Mrs. Hornell's staff. If so, how would I survive a regular church environment? Was I supposed to accept the way we were treated? I felt guilty for thinking this way and I quickly repented.

It was a good thing that Mrs. Hornell felt the need to spend more time with us after Ms. Albertson left, because no one would have noticed—or cared—how badly Ms. Marci treated us. The truth is, I became somewhat numb to it; her abuse was so constant and pervasive that it seemed almost normal. I knew that no one would believe me anyway, even if I were to speak up.

I clung to Mrs. Hornell every chance I got. Even though I didn't agree with her most of the time, I still loved her and wanted to please her. I felt like a child starved for affection. I recognized that Mrs. Hornell cared and I wanted to cling to that. I discovered years later that she had reprimanded Ms. Marci repeatedly for making fun of me publicly and yelling at me in a ridiculing way. Ms. Marci failed to heed Mrs. Hornell's warnings to change her abusive behavior, and she was finally given the choice of apologizing to me or leaving the program. She left and, thank God, I never saw her again.

The most positive lesson I learned from my interactions with Ms. Marci was that I was hearing from

God more than I realized before her arrival. Unfortunately, I fought that realization, even after receiving Jesus into my heart and being filled with the Holy Spirit. Mrs. Hornell and the staff treated me like a thieving drug abuser and, sadly, I felt deserving of their treatment.

I wanted to tell my parents about everything going on at the program, but I was so indoctrinated, that it felt *normal*! This was how my life was *supposed* to be and I was simply being ungrateful. It would have been impossible to tell my parents in any case, because the staff monitored every phone call. I had become cautious and wary of everyone. I was not the same person who arrived at the center nearly two years earlier. I had grown in many ways, but my parents had no opportunity to recognize the changes. I concluded that I had put myself in this predicament and I deserved it.

"Never be afraid to trust an unknown future to a known God."

Corrie ten Boom

8

Guarded

Watch over your heart with all diligence, for from it flows the springs of life. (Proverbs 4:23)

I grew to love some of the girls I lived with and I wanted to protect them, especially from Ms. Scareton. I also wanted to give new girls coming into the program the chance I never had to grow and flourish. Before graduation, I mentioned the idea of joining the staff to Mrs. Hornell. Surprisingly, she reacted enthusiastically and she agreed to begin my training after graduation. When I told my parents, they were as proud and excited as I was. This was a big step! I was being promoted. Finally, things were looking up for me.

≈≈≈≈≈≈

I liked Ms. Lexy and Ms. Cassey, the newest staff members. Ms. Lexy was soft and kind, unlike Ms. Scareton, and she brought order to everything. I could tell that she loved the Lord and strived to please Him. Ms. Cassey, who joined the staff after Ms. Lexy, came straight from a bible college in Dallas, Texas. She was loud and enthusiastic about everything, and her hair was as big as the state she came from. She brought a wonderful sense of fun into the program. Her eyes danced even when she wasn't talking. Ms. Cassey was refreshing to watch because she worked with an enthusiasm and joy that I had not seen much of since I arrived at the school.

Ms. Lexy and Ms. Cassey had very different personalities and were interesting to watch. I hardly noticed Ms. Scareton, who was gone more...and that was fine with me.

Mrs. Hornell invited a few of us to visit her family and to minister in Oklahoma, just weeks before graduation. I felt honored to be chosen to visit. The idea of meeting Mrs. Hornell's family and friends, and seeing where she grew up was intriguing. I was also nervous about the trip; usually the girls sang together, but this time I would sing by myself. I was grateful not to have to talk about my past, however; just a little "song and dance" to please the crowd.

The girls who were chosen to make the trip with Mrs. Hornell were my closest friends and we had been together since my first day. Ms. Cassey came along too, and she made even a nauseating car ride fun. After two days, we arrived at Mrs. Hornell's sister's house, in time for a family reunion. A handful of people were already at the house that was no bigger than a two-bedroom apartment. It was going to be very cozy! We arrived late in the evening and sleep came easily after the long ride.

The next day, we helped with whatever was needed to prepare for the reunion. I was put in charge of making sure that tables and chairs were out and ready to be used. Some of the other girls prepared food and beverages. We greeted the huge family as everyone arrived, and helped with whatever needed to be done. I fought off the feeling of exhaustion because I wanted to meet Mrs. Hornell's mother when she arrived. I was excited when we were introduced, and we quickly became engrossed in conversation outside on the patio.

After about 30 minutes of conversation with Mrs. Hornell's mother, I desperately needed to take a short nap. I ran inside to ask Mrs. Hornell's permission. As I made my way inside the house, I couldn't find her anywhere. The house was so packed with people that it was hard to maneuver through the rooms and hallways. I made my way through the kitchen to the living room. Just as I was about to enter the living room, I saw Mrs.

Hornell walking toward me. I was surprised by the hard, angry look on her face. I wondered what could be wrong.

"Taylor!" Mrs. Hornell demanded, without asking any questions, "Why were you going in there when you *knew* they were watching an R-rated movie?" She had assumed that I had something to do with a situation about which I knew nothing at all. I was shocked, but I had become so conditioned to say nothing that I did not respond to her accusation.

I thought, "Why would I would break the rules and be devious?" I thought Mrs. Hornell trusted me. I felt hurt. Had I known that an R-rated movie was playing, I would never have gone near the room. I knew then, looking at her all too familiar expression, Mrs. Hornell was not someone with whom God intended for me to be close. To her, I would always be the troubled girl who came up the snowy mountain road two and a half years ago. It was heartbreaking and, for the first time in a long time, I wanted to run far away. It was clear that further growth would only be possible beyond the program. I knew that no matter what I did, it would never be good enough for Mrs. Hornell or anyone else.

I became more disgusted and bitter than ever before in my time at the center. I felt truly alone. When was God going to come to my defense? When was God going to open Mrs. Hornell's eyes? When would my new day come? "Where are You, Lord?" I cried. That was when I fell in love with Psalm 28:7-8:

> *The LORD is my strength and my shield;*
> *My heart trusts in Him, and I am helped;*
> *Therefore my heart exults, and with my song I shall thank Him.*
> *The LORD is their strength, and He is a saving defense to His anointed.*

Holding to this scripture, I knew that my day of salvation *would* come and I *would* be defended. I held on to His truth and waited for His help to come.

The incident at Mrs. Hornell's sister's house broke my heart and I lost all respect for her. I had grown to trust Mrs. Hornell more than anyone else, since Ms. Sundry left. I decided to leave the center as soon as I graduated.

"It is not my ability, but my response to God's ability, that counts."

Corrie ten Boom

9

God's Ability

*"For I know the plans that I have for you," declares
the LORD, "plans for welfare and not for calamity, to
give you a future and a hope."* (Jeremiah 29:11)

I was graduating! I finally heard the words I had been
longing to hear from my parents on our last phone
call: "We're proud of you!" I picked out my dress for
the long-awaited event...my big day!

The center hosted a banquet in the city once a year as
a fundraiser. Most of our annual support came from this
event, so it was hugely important. Hundreds of people
came from the surrounding area to see the girls perform.
It was nerve racking, because in addition to our
performances, a graduation ceremony would be included.
My dad had been transferred to Italy by the military the
previous summer. It was too expensive for my whole
family to make the trip to see me graduate, so my mother
came alone.

The night I thought never would come finally arrived! I was the only graduate out of all the girls who were in the program when I started! One or two girls from my class had more work to complete, but at least they were still in the program! Other girls I knew had packed their bags and quit at various times. I wished that they could have graduated with me. I missed them now, and I resented Ms. Scareton and Ms. Albertson even more, because I knew that they had driven those girls away.

Girls who quit the program had to work toward their GED's after they left, because leaving the program early made some credits non-transferrable. My helper, , left the program with only three weeks left before she would have graduated. I watched her seem to wither away after Ms. Albertson ran off. All of Rachel's work was wasted!

But here I was, a high school graduate!

For three months we prepared for the big banquet. There were many songs to memorize and our testimonies had to be perfect. The weeks leading up to the banquet seemed to run together.

All the girls piled into the school's big red Suburban for the short ride to the event. We did not have traditional caps and gowns, so I wore a new black and white dress that I had chosen for my BIG day. I was excited about graduating in front of everyone. Many would have attended other banquets and would have seen me since I began the program. I felt accomplished and proud. I wanted the whole world to know that I was a good, hard working person, *and* a High School Graduate!

After the dinner, Mrs. Hornell introduced me as the new graduate. She spoke about my accomplishments in the program and in school. I was surprised when her voice began to break, and she cried as she shared her impressions during our first phone interview—the one I couldn't remember—and about how much I had changed since then. I wondered if her tears were because she knew what I had suffered in the program or because she was surprised and gratified that I hadn't quit. Perhaps they were tears of joy. I couldn't be sure, but I had a feeling that her tears were a combination of all those feelings.

The moment came for me to receive my diploma. As Mrs. Hornell invited me to the front, over 100 people stood and clapped...just for me! A standing ovation; something I never expected and it was almost overwhelming. I loved seeing how proud my mother looked. I felt all of heaven clapping too. I had nothing more to prove, because my hard work had done it for me. Suddenly, all the effort it took to go through the program felt completely worthwhile. Ultimately, it was for Jesus that I stood before what seemed like all heaven and earth. In my heart I knew He was smiling and nothing else mattered.

When the event was over, all the pictures had been taken, and the last person had left, our efforts to make the banquet a success had raised enough money for the school to operate for a long time.

≈≈≈≈≈≈

I was excited about spending a week with my mother after graduation, and I was thrilled to have a break from the strict schedule of the school. Mom and I had shared brief visits throughout my time in the program, but we needed concentrated, quality time together. I wanted her to feel safe and confident that I was a different person as a result of my experience. We would need every minute of our week together to begin building the friendship that I imagined other mothers and daughters enjoyed. It would be important to share completely my experience at the program with Mom. I had a feeling she sensed that things at the center were not as they seemed. So much could accomplish by having conversations that were not monitored.

We drove from the center to my former home town, where my mother's best friend lived, who had told Mom about the ministry center two and a half years earlier. I was no longer the same girl and I felt like I held an unconscious shield around my heart as we drove through town to my old neighborhood. We stayed only a few hours before making our way to a hotel.

The subject of my "cheating" incident came up during the week with my mother. She had been given no details by the center's staff when the incident occurred, and she was left with an impression that something was not right about it. I was surprised and relieved that she had sensed there was more to the incident than she had been told. I wanted just to pour out everything in my heart to her, but so many emotions were going through me at once that I had trouble focusing.

After the experiences of the past two and a half years, I was not sure that *anyone* was trustworthy. Sadly, I had grown so paranoid that I believed my own mother could be setting me up only to be slapped down. As crazy as that sounds, that's how I felt about everyone. It helped me to see her genuine concern, and I so *wanted* to trust her.

Awkwardly, I put on my "smile" and changed the subject from the cheating incident. Mom saw through my feeble attempt to change the subject, but she was gracious enough not to bring it up again. A few years later, when I could no longer endure keeping my experiences bottled up inside me, my mother's friendship helped propel my healing forward.

Our week together passed all too quickly. I knew that I would miss her terribly, but I also knew I had to go back to the center and complete my assignment there. I also did not trust anyone in charge to look after the well-being of others who were still in the program. I wanted the girls who remained to share my overpowering joy of knowing that the experience was worth the price. Perhaps they could also learn that nothing is impossible with the support of my Friend, Jesus…nothing!

*"Faith is like radar that sees through the fog-
the reality of things at a distance that the human
eye cannot see."*

Corrie ten Boom

10

Faith
and the Human Eye

*I have been crucified with Christ; and it is no longer I
who live, but Christ lives in me; and the life which I now
live in the flesh I live by faith in the Son of God,
who loved me and gave Himself up for me.*

(Galatians 2:20)

Mrs. Hornell started training me to be a staff member during the week before graduation. I had not shared my struggle with her about leaving the school for good. Even though I wanted to help other girls to grow and flourish, I had come to the school for healing in my life; I was only now in a position for that to begin. I prayed for my Friend to show me His view and desire for me.

After returning from my week off, following graduation, Mrs. Hornell assigned a house and a group of girls for me to oversee. I was more than a little curious about the staff quarters, which had been off limits for two and a half years. I also had normal phone privileges, without anyone monitoring my conversations. The best part of being on staff was that Ms. Scareton had no more authority over me. I rarely saw her, since I was in charge of the other group of girls in the center's second cottage.

I loved my group of girls and I could tell they loved me. Private conversations and personal relationships between students were forbidden, to prevent two or more already troubled girls from feeding off one another's negativity. As a staff member, I felt free to know the girls on a more intimate level. Talking and praying with them one-on-one was wonderful.

It was hard for me to grasp my new authority. The girls asked me for permission to do everything, just like I had done as a student. No one seemed frightened of me and it was great to see the girls being themselves and enjoying life. I loved taking care of them and helping them heal.

I was excited about helping a new student who would arrive soon. Protecting her in this environment would be tough; I would not always be around to watch out for her. I also knew I could give any situation I couldn't control to my Friend, Jesus. He *always* knew what to do.

I checked Cindy's bags when she arrived. Everything a new student brought with her had to be checked, for her own protection and for everyone's safety. I knew it was important, yet I felt like I was violating her life and privacy. I wanted everything to be normal and peaceful, but this place lacked both of those qualities. I could tell that Cindy sensed the uneasy atmosphere. She was extremely thin from years of drug use; she looked like she needed a good meal and a few weeks of sleep. My heart broke for her and I was certain I could relate to whatever her experiences had been.

The first day for a new student was always highly stressful, as every sense of what was once familiar was rapidly erased. That night, I assigned Cindy a helper, and after everything was unpacked and put away, we all sat in the living room for "family devotions." In an effort to make Cindy's first day as comfortable as possible, I thought family devotions would be easier for her to adjust to than plunging into private devotions. I wanted her to have a sense that we were a family (at least when I was on duty). I could not tell whether my plan worked, because Cindy's whole body looked as stressed as anyone I had ever seen.

I loved family devotion times, because the girls could voice their perceptions in a place where personal opinions were otherwise unwelcome, looked down upon, or forbidden. In a sense, family devotion times helped to set the girls free. I pretended that they were my daughters living in my own house. It was fun!

≈≈≈≈≈≈

I was the teacher on duty for the classroom during Cindy's first full day. I gave her all the orientation worksheets, which would help acquaint her with everything about the school program. I sat with her, making sure she understood everything and I tried hard to make the worksheets less overwhelming. It seemed to put a little ease into her sad eyes. That night, everyone got ready for bed and we had our family devotions. We all tried to make sure that she felt loved and accepted.

I awoke the following morning to get the girls ready for school and discovered that Cindy was GONE! I ran through the house, while the other girls looked on, mystified. I hoped desperately that Cindy was in one of the rooms. I tried telling myself that she must be wandering around somewhere. I ran to the back of the house and discovered the door that had been locked was wide open! My heart sank as I realized that Cindy had run away.

I was in shock but, amazingly, I didn't cry. I called Mrs. Hornell to tell her what had happened and she came right over. I could not help wondering what I had done wrong to make Cindy run away. Deep down, I could not blame her and I hoped she was safe. Weeks later, we learned that before Cindy had arrived, she made plans with a friend to meet if things weren't working out. Cindy had run down to the main road, sometime during the night, where her friend was waiting to pick her up.

It broke my heart that Cindy missed a chance to experience the kind of friendship I had with Jesus. I wanted her to have that relationship with Him, because at least *that* part of being in the program was real. I hoped Cindy felt His warmth and presence during the short time she was with us. I hoped that she felt loved, because I knew that she came from a home that had none.

≈≈≈≈≈≈

During my off-duty time, I shared a small cottage with Ms. Cassey who, at one point, I had grown to trust. She was young, carefree, and never seemed judgmental of anyone...or so I thought. I confided in her once, hoping for prayer support. Less than five minutes later, I overheard her telling Ms. Lexy, in front of the other girls, every detail of what I had shared in confidence. I learned to hold my thoughts, feelings, and concerns to myself around her, just as I had learned to do with the other staff members.

My alone times in the staff quarters were especially enjoyable. I had not been by myself in almost three years, since students were never allowed to be alone, for protective reasons. It was wonderful to be surrounded by peace and quiet. On my time off, I often walked through the forest and wrote prayers to my Friend. I loved and admired His creation in this wilderness. I felt His warmth and presence walking next to me. I could even tell whether He was on my left or right side as we walked together. It was blissful! I loved knowing that Jesus was my best Friend, who knew all my secrets and *kept* them. He also shared secrets with me and I learned to distinguish His voice from the other voices with which I seemed to be constantly at war. When He talked with me, my heart always felt light, compared to the heaviness of guilt and condemnation that I often battled. Jesus was my only source of real peace, and I loved Him.

One day, my Friend said that Mr. and Mrs. Hornell's marriage was in trouble. He told me to pray for them regularly. Once a week, the staff met with Mrs. Hornell to discuss the students' progress and other routine issues, and we always started the meetings with prayer. On the day I was asked to lead the prayer, my Friend told me to pray for Mr. and Mrs. Hornell's marriage. Without thinking twice, I began to pray. After I finished, Mrs. Hornell said, "So *you're* the one who's been praying for us! No wonder our marriage is doing so much better." From the look on her face I could tell that she was surprised. Mrs. Hornell never shared with anyone what she was going through in her marriage or anything about her personal life. I had no direct knowledge that her marriage was under attack; I only had my Friend's direction to pray for them. He knew what was going on, and I was honored that He trusted me with the secret.

I loved meeting with my Friend and I loved having an empty house, where I could escape the busyness of the school. I looked forward to looking over my weekly schedule, detailing times when I was on duty with the girls and when I had time to myself. I felt like a responsible adult.

I loved taking short naps in the afternoons when I was off duty. I looked forward to sleep because my Friend visited me there. As I fell asleep one afternoon, an image came to mind that was as clear as if someone had put a television screen in front of my face. The image began at the entrance of a room, near a front door, where a man walked in with a white sheet covering his entire body.

Although I could not see his face, I knew that he was focused on a mission. I was paralyzed with fear as he walked straight toward me and jumped on top of my chest, knocking my breath out. He was strong and all of his weight lay directly on my chest. In my mind, I screamed for my Friend to help. I tried to say His name, but nothing would come out and I knew that was exactly the man's plan. Seconds felt like minutes; I couldn't tell how much time went by before my Friend's beautiful name escaped my lips. "JEEEESSSSSSSSUSSSS!" I gasped. Immediately, the man vanished and I could breathe again. I lay there with my eyes shut tight, too scared to move. I knew the man was gone, but would he return? Was he in the room watching me? I didn't know. All I knew for sure was that I had experienced something very dark and far beyond my understanding.

As soon as I was able to move, I ran to the main cottage and stayed there for the night with everyone else. I was in a state of semi-shock and my chest still felt tight from the fear that had paralyzed me. I wanted to block everything that had happened from my mind. I did not know what to think of the encounter, and I had no one to talk to about it. I wanted to tell Mrs. Hornell, but I did not trust her and I feared her reaction, as if I had done something to deserve the horrible dream. Similar visions had occurred before I came to the school, but I thought they were over and that I had closed every door to my past. The difference now was that I had my Friend to protect and save me. Feeling His presence stronger than ever, my chest loosened. I knew He was close and I trusted that. I thought about how powerful His name was when I was able to speak it. I put the experience and my thoughts in a box and gave them to my Friend. I knew that He could heal anything!

"If you look at the world, you'll be distressed. If you look within, you'll be depressed. If you look at God you'll be at rest."

Corrie ten Boom

11

REST

And He said, "My presence shall go with you, and I will give you rest." (Exodus 33:14)

A ministry trip was planned for four girls and me to visit a small, quaint church with about 50 people, located in the city near the school. I liked the intimacy of the setting, where we could talk and pray personally with each person in the congregation. I loved the freedom to be led by the Lord and minister to whomever He directed me. I was also relieved not to have to give my testimony.

After our performance, Mrs. Hornell spoke about marriage. Before inviting married couples to come for prayer, she gave a testimonial about how God had helped her own marriage. I was shocked when she mentioned my name and told everyone that God had placed an anointing on me to pray for couples. She said she knew my prayers had helped her crumbling marriage, because she had told no one about it. Mrs. Hornell went on to speak about how she discovered, during a staff meeting, that I had been praying for her and how God used me. I was stunned by how much my prayers had touched Mrs. Hornell. I don't remember what I prayed for her marriage; only that Jesus told me to pray.

Mrs. Hornell shocked me even more by asking me to come forward and pray for everyone. I begged God to help me as I walked toward the front of the church. I told Him I wasn't ready for this; I didn't deserve this kind of privilege. I asked, "What am I going to say, Lord? Please give me the words. I don't know what to do. PLEASE help me!" My heart broke as a long line of couples formed. Seeing so many people in so much pain compelled me to ask God for their miracle, and I recalled this scripture:

> *When they bring you before the synagogues and the rulers and the authorities, do not worry about how or what you are to speak in your defense, or what you are to say, for the Holy Spirit will teach you in that very hour what you ought to say.* (Luke 12:11-12)

One couple after another came for me to lift their marriage to heaven and pray for their breakthrough. Jesus knew what to say when I didn't, and I was at peace with that. I knew I would never see those precious people again, so I prayed that God would touch each couple in a way I could not. By the time we got back to the school, I was exhausted and sleep came easily.

When I awoke and went to the main house for something to eat, I heard that Mrs. Hornell wanted me to call her immediately. I felt a little sick, because Mrs. Hornell never called just to say, "Hi." After taking a moment to prepare myself, I dialed her number. Maybe the "troubled girl" label was starting to wear off and I was someone who mattered.

When Mrs. Hornell answered the phone, I was surprised and relieved to discover that she was not concerned about me. She had come to the conclusion that Ms. Scareton was involved in something shady. Mrs. Hornell did not share anything specific about her suspicions, but she instructed me to make certain that Ms. Scareton did not stop by a local tanning salon when we picked up food donations the following morning. Mrs. Hornell asked me to keep an eye on Ms. Scareton and report back to her. Ms. Scareton was already on some kind of probation, about which I knew nothing, and her job at the school was in jeopardy unless something changed, whatever it was.

I did not know what specifically to watch for, except to observe Ms. Scareton and keep her away from the tanning salon. Mrs. Hornell's conversation confirmed the feelings I had, almost since I arrived at the school, that something was not right about Ms. Scareton.

The next morning, I traveled the familiar route with Ms. Scareton to pick up food donations. We knew the route by heart. We met the same people at the same place and on the same day every week. This was the only errand that day, but Ms. Scareton turned in the opposite direction from the way we should have gone to return to the school. "OH, MY GOD!" I thought, "Where is she going?" I was frightened of Ms. Scareton, and I kept quiet. I did not yet know what she had in mind or of what she was capable. I knew she lied about me and other girls to Mrs. Hornell. I suspected she might do anything to protect herself, while throwing me into the "lion's den."

Ms. Scareton pulled into the parking lot of the tanning salon I had been warned specifically to keep her from entering. "I'll be right back," she said. I sat, still and silent, as she carried a plain envelope into the salon. I didn't know what to do. I was supposed to stop her, but how? The voices in my mind were at war. I wanted to run after her and tell her that whatever she was doing was wrong, but I was paralyzed with the same fear that had seized me whenever I was around her. I hated that feeling. I wished for the courage and authority to stop her, but I watched silently as she walked into the salon.

I could see everything going on through the glass door. Ms. Scareton exchanged simple nods and gestures with a man to whom she handed the envelope. The quick meeting had obviously been planned. She was clearly involved in *something* improper. I felt sick as I watched the scene play out and I prayed for God to protect me.

When Ms. Scareton got back in the car, I managed to ask, "Didn't Mrs. Hornell tell you not to go into that place?" I felt even sicker than before, my hands felt clammy, and I was shaking. Ms. Scareton made a nervous gesture, rubbed her nose, and mumbled something I couldn't understand. Sitting only a few inches away from her, I could tell my question had caught her off guard. The ride home was silent and anxious. I knew that I had to report to Mrs. Hornell everything that had happened. The irony was thick: Ms. Scareton and I had reversed our roles; now *I* was watching *her*!

I didn't even think to help unload the car when we arrived back at the school. I made a dash for the office, not stopping to knock on the door. Ms. Lexy was working in the office as I rushed in with a panicked look on my face. I was so scared that all I could say was that I needed to talk to Mrs. Hornell right away. Ms. Lexy asked me if I was okay, but I couldn't answer her. I was running out of time; Ms. Scareton could not be far behind, and she would throw me "under the bus" to save herself if I didn't talk to Mrs. Hornell first.

"I need to talk to Mrs. Hornell, NOW," I gasped. "It's an emergency!" As soon as Ms. Lexy gave me the phone, Ms. Scareton burst into the office. I had never before seen fear like that in her eyes.

"I need to...to talk to...Mrs. Hornell," Ms. Scareton stuttered. Ms. Lexy told her to leave and, surprisingly, Ms. Scareton walked out, looking like a dog that had been whipped. Ms. Lexy dialed Mrs. Hornell, who was at home not far from the school. Even though I felt relieved just hearing her voice, she could hear the panic still in mine. It took several minutes to give Mrs. Hornell every detail of Ms. Scareton's passing an envelope to an unknown man at the tanning salon.

"Did you see what was in the envelope, Taylor?" Mrs. Hornell asked. "By the way," she continued before I could answer, "WHY DID YOU LET HER GO INTO THE SALON?" Her tone was angry and her voice made me feel anxious.

I responded quickly, "I didn't know *what* to do and I told her she wasn't *supposed* to go in there, but she just mumbled something I couldn't understand." My words fell out in a jumbled mess. I felt that I had let Mrs. Hornell down...again...and I wished that I had done *something* to stop Ms. Scareton. Deep down, however, I knew that I was not prepared for that battle.

When Mrs. Hornell had sorted through all the details, she said, finally, "You are going to stay on the phone while I deal with Dominique."

"My God," I thought, "How awkward is this going to be?" Mrs. Hornell told Ms. Lexy to get Ms. Scareton back in the office for a conference call. Mrs. Hornell's voice became progressively louder over the speakerphone and I felt very uncomfortable as Ms. Scareton started to cry, looking at me briefly in total embarrassment.

I wanted to hang up the phone, run inside my house, and pretend nothing had happened. I survived my most difficult times in the program through denial. I was good at pretending there wasn't a problem in the world. Each time I refused to deal with reality, like during the conference call with Ms. Scareton and Mrs. Hornell, It felt as if some of my self was lost. I was relieved that, because of my scheduled duties with the girls, she and I would not be staying in the same house that night.

God showed me how strong He was making me, even through the latest experience with Ms. Scareton, and that

He "had my back" the whole time. The faith He had been building in me was working, even when I was shaking in fear. I saw how wonderful it was to trust Him, and what that trust produced when I endured through even the toughest experience. If I had left immediately after graduating, like some girls, I would have missed His demonstration of deliverance, abounding love, and mercy for me.

"*Faith sees the invisible, believes the unbelievable, and receives the impossible.*"

Corrie ten Boom

12

Receiving the Impossible

And without faith it is impossible to please Him, for he who comes to God must believe that He is and that He is a rewarder of those who seek Him. (Hebrews 11:6)

I n the week following the tanning salon incident, Ms. Scareton stopped being aggressive and mean toward me and the other girls. In fact, she never bothered anyone after the confrontation with Mrs. Hornell, until the day she was asked to leave. It was as if God had shut her mouth like He did with the lions' mouths for Daniel in the Old Testament.

> *Then the king gave orders, and Daniel was brought in and cast into the lions' den. The king spoke and said to Daniel, "Your God whom you constantly serve will Himself deliver you"*
>
> *A stone was brought and laid over the mouth of the den; and the king sealed it with his own signet ring and*

with the signet rings of his nobles, so that nothing would be changed in regard to Daniel.

Then the king went off to his palace and spent the night fasting, and no entertainment was brought before him; and his sleep fled from him.

Then the king arose at dawn, at the break of day, and went in haste to the lions' den.

When he had come near the den to Daniel, he cried out with a troubled voice. The king spoke and said to Daniel, "Daniel, servant of the living God, has your God, whom you constantly serve, been able to deliver you from the lions?"

Then Daniel spoke to the king, "O king, live forever!

"My God sent His angel and shut the lions' mouths and they have not harmed me, inasmuch as I was found innocent before Him; and also toward you, O king, I have committed no crime."

Then the king was very pleased and gave orders for Daniel to be taken up out of the den. So Daniel was taken up out of the den and no injury whatever was found on him, because he had trusted in his God. (Daniel 6:16-23)

While fixing a leaky faucet one day, Mr. Hornell found a bottle of wine hidden under the sink in the staff quarters. Ms. Scareton confessed that she had been drinking on the job. I never knew all the details of Ms. Scareton's termination, but I gathered that more than drinking was responsible. Once she was gone, I felt that I could begin fully healing. I found a scripture that gave me confidence to walk through and over anything:

"For I will restore you to health, and I will heal you of your wounds," declares the LORD, "Because they have called you an outcast, saying: 'It is Zion; no one cares for her.'" (Jeremiah 30:17)

A combination of shock and relief moved across the girls' faces when they learned that Ms. Scareton had left the school. My heart felt as light as their expressions. The whole energy changed in a moment, as a great burden lifted. We all cried with relief and felt ready to press forward. The experience of being around Ms. Scareton for three years reminded me of the scripture in the book of Proverbs:

When the righteous increase, the people rejoice, but when a wicked man rules, people groan. (Proverbs 29:2)

It felt as though God had finally heard my cry for help. I couldn't have been more grateful and more in love with Him than I was in that moment.

You have taken account of my wanderings; put my tears in Your bottle. Are they not in Your book?
(Psalm 56:8)

Hear my prayer, O LORD, and give ear to my cry; do not be silent at my tears; for I am a stranger with You, a sojourner like all my fathers. (Psalm 39:12)

The LORD is near to all who call upon Him, to all who call upon Him in truth. He will fulfill the desire of those who fear Him; He will also hear their cry and will save them. (Psalm 145:18-19)

After Ms. Scareton was gone, it became very clear how distorted things had been and how much better life could be for everyone with Jesus as Lord. New students were continually arriving, but many quit early and that did not need to happen. God seemed to trust me to invest my faith and experience in the precious lives of His children. Hearing His voice and seeing His view of His daughters was an incredible blessing. I became a surrogate parent overnight, and the accountability was awesome, because I knew He was the one who had put me in my position.

I wanted to do everything I could to help the girls heal in the way they most needed. I had charge of five girls and grew quite close to them. I held them in my heart and I couldn't have been more proud of them! I told them so every day, because most of them had never received any positive encouragement before they came to the school. I wanted to set a standard of complete openness with them, so that they would feel safe confiding in me. They had been through enough!

When I was a student, I needed help to know how to clean properly, and I resented being accused of laziness in completing my chores. I knew that everyone saw through different eyes, with different personalities, and they had different ways of thinking. I tried to assure each girl that she could be her best without being compared to anyone else. I knew I was making a difference in their lives when they were excited to see me after I returned from being off duty for a couple of days. One girl said that she loved when I came to work and she missed me when I wasn't there. It was one thing to *believe* that I was making a difference in their lives; it was another thing to *know* it!

≈≈≈≈≈≈

I asked a lot of questions as a staff member. As a student, I did not have that freedom. I wanted to see to it that the girls who followed me were given the best chance to ask questions, to speak, and to defend themselves. For example, when one of the girls demonstrated a "bad attitude," I simply asked her if she was okay and let her share her heart, rather than bashing her and demanding that she straighten up. Amazingly, attitudes turned around almost instantly. The smallest courtesies or caring gestures accomplished more than all the verbal abuse and punishment that had been the pattern. In many cases, a little encouragement and a hug were often all that was needed to make the biggest difference.

I developed a policy of dealing with no one until the facts were known about a particular matter. My experience as a student taught me much about the dangers of making assumptions. The girls did not need more judgment to weigh them down; they deserved equal and fair treatment. The foundation for my relationship with them was that we are all children of God in the eyes of our Heavenly Father, nothing less. I cherished the thought that God trusted me to care for His kids and I didn't want to let Him down.

Jesus called for them, saying, "Permit the children to come to Me, and do not hinder them, for the kingdom of God belongs to such as these." (Luke 18:16)

I respected the fact that the girls *wanted* to change and grow, so I did whatever I could to help them succeed. It was important for me to recognize that each one's perception of life was uniquely hers. I had already learned, through painful experiences in the program, that judgment crushes a person's spirit.

When I was still a student, I overheard a confrontation between a staff member and another student who had been accused by one of the girls of being rude and hurtful. I had witnessed the incident and I saw nothing of the kind in the accused girl's behavior. Without attempting to gather facts or seek input from anyone, the staff member summarily reprimanded the girl. It broke my heart that she was disciplined wrongly.

I wanted the girls to feel comfortable with how God had created and ordained each of them uniquely. I kept this perspective in my heart, together with whatever wisdom I had gained through my experience in the program. I hoped that I was helping make the girls' lives better. More importantly, I hoped that I was making God smile; ultimately, that was what mattered to me the most.

I saw my Friend's providential hand upon me increase as the weeks and months progressed. His presence became more real to me day by day. Even though I struggled at times to hear His voice, I always knew when He was near. I often found it difficult to come back to reality after being in prayer, like coming out of a dream, but without having been asleep. The world's noises were shut off during those moments. My Friend was faithful to cover me with His love at all the right times. The idea of Him stepping down from heaven to visit me was incredibly humbling. During the most hurtful and devastating times at the school, I held on tightly to who He was to me...my Friend.

There were lonely moments too, when I didn't feel my Friend's warmth and presence around me, and I asked Him, "Why, God, Why? Where were you when I needed you? Where were you when my pillow was soaked in tears?" Ten years after I left the school, I came to understand. A dear friend told me go to Matthew's account, when God was silent even in Jesus' last hours.

> *Then Jesus came with them to a place called Gethsemane, and said to His disciples, "Sit here while I go over there and pray." And He took with Him Peter and the two sons of Zebedee, and began to be grieved and distressed.*
>
> *Then He said to them, "My soul is deeply grieved, to the point of death; remain here and keep watch with Me."*
>
> *And He went a little beyond them, and fell on His face and prayed, saying, "My Father, if it is possible, let this cup pass from Me; yet not as I will, but as You will."*
>
> *And He came to the disciples and found them sleeping, and said to Peter, "So, you men could not keep watch*

with Me for one hour? Keep watching and praying that you may not enter into temptation; the spirit is willing, but the flesh is weak."

He went away again a second time and prayed, saying, "My Father, if this cannot pass away unless I drink it, Your will be done."

Again He came and found them sleeping, for their eyes were heavy. And He left them again, and went away and prayed a third time, saying the same thing once more.

(Matthew 26:36-44)

About the ninth hour Jesus cried out with a loud voice, saying, "ELI, ELI, LAMA SABACHTHANI?" that is, "MY GOD, MY GOD, WHY HAVE YOU FORSAKEN ME?" (Matthew 27: 46)

God was silent when His only begotten Son would have wanted to feel His presence the most! That's when faith is tested and proven—even *"Jesus Christ's faith"* (Romans 3:22).

"*Forgiveness is the key which unlocks the door of resentment and the handcuffs of hatred. It breaks the chains of bitterness and the shackles of selfishness. The forgiveness of Jesus not only takes away our sin, it makes them as if they had never been.*"

Corrie ten Boom

13

It is Finished!

A strange feeling began working inside me that my time at the school was coming to an end. It was spring and I had graduated seven months earlier. I was scheduled to visit my family in Italy during the summer for a month and I couldn't have been more excited. I don't remember much about the time leading up to my trip, except that it was very peaceful.

When the day came for me to say goodbye to the girls, I told them not to worry; the month would pass quickly and I would be coming back. As the words passed my lips, I felt suddenly that this was a *final* goodbye. I didn't want to believe it because it wasn't in my plan; however, most of the girls were almost ready to graduate. I was so proud of them.

While walking to the main house to gather some last minute things for my trip, I noticed that Mrs. Hornell's car was already in the driveway. She was going to take me to the airport and she was always very punctual, but *never* early. I thought perhaps she had a few things to do in the office, but I saw that it was empty as I walked to the cottage. I hurried up the stairs to the staff bedroom, to make sure I had everything in order for my trip. Mrs. Hornell was waiting for me. I thought she must have wanted to get an early start to the airport, but she said she needed to speak with me. I sat on one of the beds as Mrs. Hornell got on her knees in front of me. She said she knew that some of the staff had been mean and abusive during my stay at the center. She begged me not to repeat the same patterns of behavior with the girls for whom I was responsible. I was the only one left out of all the girls who were in the program when I arrived. Mrs. Hornell said that she had wanted to have this conversation with me sooner, but had been unable to broach the subject any sooner.

I sat there shocked! Was Mrs. Hornell trying to apologize? Was she admitting her role in the abuse her staff had perpetrated? Did she hope I would forgive and forget? Why was she confessing this now? Why was she concerned that *I* would become abusive like the others? I wondered if Mrs. Hornell was afraid that I would expose her and the "ministry" as a cult-like fraud. Maybe the fact that I was leaving had convicted her of her culpability in the abuse that had occurred under her supervision. It seemed that Mrs. Hornell had suddenly realized that she *supported* the women who had literally destroyed lives in what was supposed to be a divinely-inspired ministry.

Although I understood that hurt people hurt others, it never made sense to me that Mrs. Hornell condoned the pain her staff inflicted on the girls who were ultimately in *her* care.

When she was finished, I said, "Mrs. Hornell, I could never be like those women! I cannot imagine behaving that way toward anyone! Please don't ever think that I would do the same things they did; it's not in me!"

I guess Mrs. Hornell heard whatever it was that she needed, because she changed the subject and we left for the airport. I felt confused by the conversation and a little paranoid about what the backlash might be. I did not understand Mrs. Hornell's motives, but I left it all behind me with a quick goodbye before stepping onto the plane.

I resigned myself to the fact that I could not prove myself any more than I already had, to Mrs. Hornell or anyone else. Maybe no one else would *ever* see me the way Jesus does, as a "*new creation*" (Galatians 6:15). I dreamed of being where no one knew me; where I could be everything that God has called me to be; where I could be free!

≈≈≈≈≈≈

After landing in Italy, I felt exhilarated, like I had been under water for the past three and a half years and I could breathe air for the first time! I did not realize the extent of the suffocation I had been feeling.

The month was filled with sightseeing and making new friends at the church my parents attended on the base where my dad was stationed. It felt good to do whatever was on God's heart, not limited by a daily schedule that no longer fit. It was only to Him—my Friend—that I was accountable. I thoroughly enjoyed the unfettered freedom I experienced in Italy. I felt like the new person I had dreamed of being, once liberated from the school.

I wanted to stay with my family in Italy and never return to "that place." My family and I were complete now. As the days moved closer to my return to the States, I had a sick feeling that I could not shake. Finally, I spoke to my mother about how I felt. We had grown close over the past three weeks and I wanted to see how she felt about me staying, before I talked to my dad. I don't remember the details of the conversation, but I do recall how wonderful I felt to hear both Mom and Dad say that they *wanted* me to stay with them and wished I had moved home sooner! I felt like I could fly! I felt a long awaited sense of release. I was free never to return to Mrs. Hornell's center!

The words Jesus spoke on the cross in His final moments, kept coming to mind: *"It is finished!"* (John 19:30). I didn't question that voice for a second, because I knew it well; the Voice that sent rivers of living water into the recesses of my desert heart. It was the wonderful, familiar, and welcome Voice of my Friend.

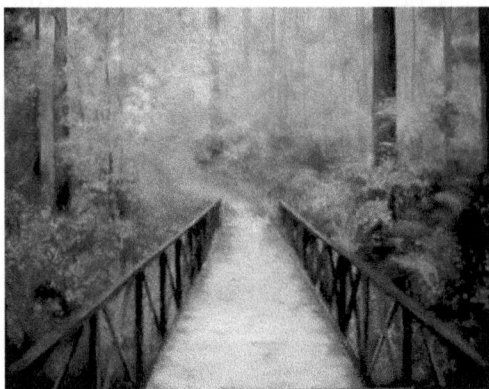

"*You can never learn that Christ is all you need, until Christ is all you have.*"

Corrie ten Boom

14

Bridge to Victory

After living in Italy for six months, I was accepted into a one-year seminary school in Rockford, Illinois. Meanwhile, my parents moved to Virginia where my dad was stationed at the Pentagon. I was searching desperately for answers to questions about my experience at the center. I still believed I *deserved* everything that had happened. I could not accept that Mrs. Hornell and her staff had acted in the name of God. I felt fearful of being rejected and considered ungrateful or disrespectful if I shared my experience, or spoke with anyone about the guilt and shame I still felt. I could not talk about, let alone resolve what had happened.

I felt like a prisoner on the inside even though I was free on the outside; a prisoner to my tears that never seemed to dry. I felt alone in my struggle to heal three and a half years of wounds. I needed victory desperately, but how could I achieve it? Where would I begin? With whom could I talk? Who would help me heal?

I had become paranoid of people and I feared their opinions of me. I did not want anyone to know about my secret prison. I wanted my parents to think I was "whole," so I remained silent, hoping my fears would go away. In the school program, I put on a façade that appeared normal to others. When I left the center, I took my façade with me, hoping it would work in the "real world."

At the center, I worked hard to gain favor with the staff, even though it seemed that I could never work hard enough to please them. I knew my Friend was not like them, yet I found myself trying to win His favor too, and working hard to earn His undivided attention. I seemed to lose my grasp of His constant and unfailing love. His presence was there, even when I messed up and expected the ground to open up and swallow me into hell. He was still in my dreams and in my ever-changing heart. He was everywhere!

I found myself sinning *on purpose*, or doing something I knew wasn't right, just to get a reaction from God, or someone else. I felt like I needed a good whipping because, well, *just because*! Years of unresolved confusion and hurt slowly began to change me into a very angry person.

For years after I left the school, the experience still hurt. I tried hard to be optimistic, grateful to God, and grounded in my faith, knowing that if it weren't for the program, I most likely would have died. Merely being alive was not good enough, however, and I continued to cry out to God for help.

My mother knew only a little of what had gone on in the program. Little by little, incidents at the school—things I had tried desperately to forget—seeped out one way or another. I hoped that my mother would understand, but what I dreaded the most happened; she refused to listen. She said it was time to stop using "that school" as an excuse for the choices I was making. I knew then she would never understand, without having been there herself. I felt hurt because I thought that, more than anyone else, she would fight to try to help me.

I wanted someone to hear me and I wanted the hurt to go away. I struggled to relate to anything except my experiences at the school. I began wondering if I was "losing it" because the memories occupied so much of my attention. WHY COULDN'T I JUST GET PAST THEM AND MOVE ON? I felt truly stuck, like it wasn't safe to talk about my experiences at all. Silence seemed to be the only solution. I was a secretive person anyway, by nature or perhaps by necessity; never the type to open up to someone. Sometimes, when I couldn't stand the desperate feeling anymore, something would come out randomly in casual conversations. I felt guilty immediately after letting something slip out, and the cycle continued. I started building walls in my mind that I decided no one would get through...no one!

As much as I loved my Friend and wanted to be everything He had called me to be, I found myself slipping away. His voice was gradually replaced by louder voices of guilt and condemnation. I was like a little girl, scared of her own shadow. I found it impossible to rest in the knowledge that Jesus loved me and that I never needed to earn His love. I couldn't tell if what I did on a daily basis pleased Him or offended Him. I condemned myself for every little sin. Now that I was out of the school, no one was accountable for my life except me! I wanted desperately to be free...completely FREE!

I knew I couldn't carry the emotional load much longer, so I began to pray for God to send me someone who truly knew and loved Him; someone I could trust and who knew nothing about my past, including the private school. I wanted my mother to be that person, but I also knew she needed the illusion that I was fine. Actually, I was afraid that she would call Mrs. Hornell to tell her that I was still a burden...still "troubled."

I didn't want to replace my Friend, but I knew there had to be someone who heard His voice and who could also help me to hear Him better. I knew there was more to life than how I was living and I wanted a *real* example to follow. I needed someone who walked their talk; who could show me the way to true freedom. I wasn't expecting perfection; I just wanted the pure truth, good or bad.

I held tightly to my Friend, even though I felt myself slipping away. I knew He was real, but I was losing hope that he would hear my prayers.

My mother found a church she liked and asked me to go with her. I was ashamed of what I had allowed myself to become and I didn't want her or anyone else to see it, so I made excuses for not going. I knew there were others who could hear my Friend's voice and I didn't want anyone to see me for who I *really* was. I just wanted to disappear. I was close to going back to my old lifestyle, and I hated myself for it.

After a few weeks, my mother invited me again to go to church with her. She said that a special speaker would be there; a minister who some called a prophet. I had read about prophets and heard about some modern ones. I had even met a few self-proclaimed prophets. To me, they were loony and weird.

Something stopped me from turning down my mother's invitation again. It was my FRIEND! I heard His voice! It was almost audible this time. He told me it was important that I go. "God, I thought I'd never hear You like that again." So, because I trusted Him, I told Mom I would meet her at the church.

I thought Sunday would never come. I was truly excited to hear what this woman had to say. I didn't have any specific expectations, but I knew the trip was full of purpose. On Sunday morning, I dropped off a friend at work and was on my way.

Metropolitan Washington, D.C. traffic is always hit or miss and this Sunday there was a parade of some kind that slowed things down. By the time I arrived at the church, half an hour late, the woman had been speaking for some time and there was a crowd of people moving toward her as she stood at the front of the church. When I finally found my mother, she had saved me a seat. The individual ministry was about to begin and something about the woman speaking felt authentic. I wanted to meet her, but I was stuck all the way in the back. By the looks of the crowd, I would never get close enough. I thought, "She's probably unreachable anyway, like most preachers."

I stayed for about 20 minutes. "Maybe I heard God wrong," I thought. Mom begged me to stay a while longer, but I left anyway. Why did I bother to come, I wondered? Just as I was about to leave, the speaker's eyes met mine. The look on her face made me feel certain instantly that somehow she knew *everything* about me! It wasn't a mean look. It was the look of a mother toward her daughter when she knew the child was up to no good. The speaker's expression frightened me and I made the fastest possible exit.

A few hours later, Mom came home and said that she had waited for the woman to pray for her and for me. My mother was the last one and was determined to speak to this woman; her name was Barbara. I loved my mom for waiting all that time just to pray for me. She could have asked for prayer about anything, but she chose to stand in the gap for me. Barbara said that she saw me inside a bottle, with a model ship in it, and that no one could touch me inside the bottle. Barbara gave my mother her phone number and said to call if I ever needed to talk. I looked at the number and thought, "I wonder how long I would have to wait to get an appointment with her?" I imagined Barbara in her big oval office with a secretary taking all her messages. I imagined that my face would blur with the rest of the people who showed up to see her. I wanted to give it a try, though, because I knew that God had wanted me to go to *that* church on *that* day. I couldn't shake the feeling that God had a plan in mind, even though I didn't know what it was.

I was very nervous about calling Barbara and leaving a message. What would I say? Where would I begin? Would I have to tell her secretary everything? Would she call me back? Would she think that what I said was even be worth her time to return my call?

I worked in a hair salon at the time and I prayed for the woman to come in. I was afraid she would rebuke me for being ungrateful or for something...*anything*. I carried her phone number around for several days. Finally, I could not ignore the feeling anymore. I picked up the phone and dialed the number. I think the phone rang twice before I heard a woman's voice. "Hello, this is Barbara," the woman answered. I couldn't believe it; it was really Barbara and not her secretary!

"Barbara? This is Barbara?" I asked.

"Yes, it is," she answered.

I couldn't believe that I was speaking directly to her. All I remember saying was, "I need your help!" I began crying, out of relief and joy. Somehow, I knew that everything was going to be okay. I don't know how I knew, but I did.

The warmth of my Friend became stronger while I talked to her. I knew this was God's way of saying, "Everything is going to be alright!"

I described to Barbara how I got her phone number and where I saw her. She said she had been waiting for me to call. I wasn't sure what she meant, but I felt a profound sense of relief and I asked if we could meet somewhere. She said her house would be fine. Before we hung up, she gave me this scripture:

> And a woman who had a hemorrhage for twelve years, and could not be healed by anyone, came up behind Him and touched the fringe of His cloak, and immediately her hemorrhage stopped.
>
> And Jesus said, "Who is the one who touched Me?"
>
> And while they were all denying it, Peter said, "Master, the people are crowding and pressing in on You."
>
> But Jesus said, "Someone did touch Me, for I was aware that power had gone out of Me."
>
> When the woman saw that she had not escaped notice, she came trembling and fell down before Him, and declared in the presence of all the people the reason why

*she had touched Him, and how she had been immediately
healed.*

*And He said to her, "Daughter, your faith has made
you well; go in peace."* (Luke 8:43-48)

Barbara said, "Just keep holding on to the hem of His
garment!"

All I could manage to say through tears was, "Thank
you!"

I was a nervous wreck when the day came to visit
Barbara, and I did not want to be one second late. I
thought that if she were going to rebuke me and call
down fire and brimstone, I didn't want to add to it by
being late! I had no idea what to expect. I kept thinking
about the laundry room at the school, where Ms.
Scareton scolded me the first time.

I was ecstatic that Barbara lived only 10 minutes away.
As I walked up to her door, I imagined two giant angels
with swords standing guard at the entrance. I began to
wonder if *my* guardian angels were that big. I almost
couldn't breathe, and it felt like it took 10 minutes to walk
five steps to her door. Finally, I rang the bell.

When Barbara answered the door, I could tell
immediately that she too knew my Friend. His presence

was everywhere in her home and it didn't feel like the laundry room at all. It was an enormous relief to feel safer than I had in a long time. She led me to her office and I was relieved again to find that, although everything had its place, it wasn't *perfect*.

We sat down and she asked how she could help me. I don't remember where I started, but I recall watching Barbara's facial expressions very carefully. She was a good listener and I appreciated that she never interrupted me. She had piercing blue eyes that seemed to look right into my soul. She didn't scare me, though; I just hoped she didn't mind all the clutter in there.

I don't think I left out a single detail about my experience at the school. I knew I wouldn't have everything figured out that day, but just unloading my story felt glorious, no matter how it came out. I didn't censor a word and I wasn't looking for sympathy; I could have gotten that from anyone. I just wanted to be free of the memories. I hoped for answers, and I trusted that Barbara would tell me the truth. I still expected her to rebuke me when I finished telling her my story; instead, her eyes looked sad, like a mother's eyes after hearing that her child had gone through an awful experience.

Finally, Barbara said, "You are called to your generation, Taylor. There are people out there with your name imprinted on their hearts and you're going to reach them!"

I never expected *that*! Barbara went on to tell me that God had given her a mother's heart for me and whatever it took to help facilitate the call of God on my life, she would do it. I was speechless. I had a hard time believing her; my experience had been the opposite for so long. She invited me to the weekly prayer meetings she held and said that I could come over anytime I needed to.

Barbara said that she felt very protective of me. It meant a lot to me because I was used to people taking advantage of my vulnerability. I wanted desperately to have a safe place to heal; to make mistakes without getting slammed for them.

Before I left her house, Barbara prayed for me, and I felt as if I lost half my body weight. As I walked to my car, I thought, "Something wonderful happened in there." Instead of carrying the usual foggy, hopeless feeling, my spiritual vision seemed to be restored. I knew I had a long way to go to heal completely, but I had begun the journey. I finally had a friend here on earth with whom I could walk.

At the first weekly meeting I attended at Barbara's house, I took the seat furthest away from her. I knew that everyone would want to be near her, but as soon as I sat down, she told me she had saved a seat for me right next to her. I was ecstatic that she *wanted* me to sit next to her! I watched Barbara as she ministered and prayed. She seemed so genuine. It was easy to be around her. I didn't have to pretend or put on a show. I sensed that she knew things about me that I had not shared with anyone. She gave me the freedom to be at peace with myself, whoever that was. I was okay with whatever the process, because I had buried the little girl long ago and I knew it would take work—and time—to bring her back.

I thank God everyday for sending Barbara into my life. Even though we've had many ups and downs over the last ten years of walking together, she has always allowed my voice to be heard, no matter what the situation or circumstance. Everything is up for discussion. There is nothing I can't talk to her about. Many times, I called her in the middle of the night for prayer and she always answered the phone. In the beginning of our relationship, I wasn't sure if sleep was on her "To Do" list.

Barbara always told me, "God doesn't have grandchildren; He has kids and lots of them." God knew I needed someone I could watch and follow, and it is in His footsteps that she walks. God knew I needed that example and I still do! I just want to walk this journey, called life, rightly.

> *"He sent from on high, He took me; He drew me out of many waters, He delivered me from my strong enemy, and from those who hated me, for they were too mighty for me.*
>
> *They confronted me in the day of my calamity,*
> *But the LORD was my stay.*
> *He brought me forth also into a broad place;*
> *He rescued me, because He delighted in me."*
>
> (Psalm 18:16-19)

To this day I hold tight to this scripture. Many times, I have found particular scriptures to be especially helpful, when I think, "Does God see me drowning? Will He rescue me from these powerful enemies that never seem to leave my side?" Yes, He will. My Friend always has, and He will do the same for you if you ask Him.

"Some knowledge is too heavy...you cannot bear it...your Father will carry it until you are able."

Corrie ten Boom

15

Judging the Fruits

You will know them by their fruits. Grapes are not gathered from thorn bushes nor figs from thistles, are they? So every good tree bears good fruit, but the bad tree bears bad fruit. A good tree cannot produce bad fruit, nor can a bad tree produce good fruit. Every tree that does not bear good fruit is cut down and thrown into the fire. So then, you will know them by their fruits. (Matthew 7:16-20)

After God restored forgiveness in my heart for the staff at the center, Mrs. Hornell called with the news that Ms. Scareton had died of a drug overdose. After she left the school, no one heard from her until her parents called to ask for prayer; she had been hospitalized after being beaten and robbed. I felt my heart break for Ms. Scareton. She had been living on the streets when she died, at only 37 years old. After hanging up the phone, I said a prayer for her family's loss, because they were hurting more than I could imagine.

I thank God for the preparation that the heartbreaking experiences I've shared in this book represent. God has brought me through everything by His grace, His mercy, and His faithfulness. It has been 14 years and quite a journey since entering the boarding school for "troubled girls." That program is part of a worldwide organization and is one of hundreds that are active today. My total experience in the program lasted less than four years, but healing its effects took many more. It was my first impression of "ministry." Although names and faces change constantly, hurting people are everywhere, even in the ministry.

Spiritual leaders throughout the world *must* be careful with God's kids. He counts every tear and needs The leaders' hands to dry them.

We seem many times to lose sight of the fact that we were all on God's mind the day He gave up His Son, Jesus, for us. We may be the only "Jesus" someone will see or know. We owe it to Him, and to all of Heaven watching, to make the day He was mocked, beaten, ridiculed, tortured, and killed worthwhile.

How long and how patient was God with you, when you were first learning to walk by faith? I pray that more spirits are being built up than are being broken down by ministries today. Are *you* building up the people with whom God has entrusted you, or are you building your own kingdom? Do your words build up or tear down those in your care? Both outcomes carry different but equally high prices.

If you are a leader—a shepherd—please read and prayerfully consider Ezekiel 34.

≈≈≈≈≈≈

Lord, I pray that You would strengthen the leaders today with Your Holy Spirit! I pray that every high wall and kingdom that is not Yours be demolished right now, in Jesus' name. You know them all by name; the ones who relish in their own power and devour Your people like hungry wolves. Bring them down, Lord, so that Your people may be brought back from their isolation and be conciliated to You. Lord, I pray that You will raise up men and women everywhere who have Your name in their hearts; people who know You and love You; whose hearts align with You and everything for which You stand.

> *But when the Son of Man comes in His glory, and all the angels with Him, then He will sit on His glorious throne. All the nations will be gathered before Him; and He will separate them from one another, as the shepherd separates the sheep from the goats; and He will put the sheep on His right, and the goats on the left.*

Then the King will say to those on His right, 'Come, you who are blessed of My Father, inherit the kingdom prepared for you from the foundation of the world.

'For I was hungry, and you gave Me something to eat; I was thirsty, and you gave Me something to drink; I was a stranger, and you invited Me in; naked, and you clothed Me; I was sick, and you visited Me; I was in prison, and you came to Me.'

Then the righteous will answer Him, 'Lord, when did we see You hungry, and feed You, or thirsty, and give You something to drink? And when did we see You a stranger, and invite You in, or naked, and clothe You? 'When did we see You sick, or in prison, and come to You?'

The King will answer and say to them, 'Truly I say to you, to the extent that you did it to one of these brothers of Mine, even the least of them, you did it to Me.'

Then He will also say to those on His left, 'Depart from Me, accursed ones, into the fire which has been prepared for the devil and his angels; for I was hungry, and you gave Me nothing to eat; I was thirsty, and you gave Me nothing to drink; I was a stranger, and you did not invite Me in; naked, and you did not clothe Me; sick, and in prison, and you did not visit Me.'

Then they themselves also will answer, 'Lord, when did we see You hungry, or thirsty, or a stranger, or naked, or sick, or in prison, and did not take care of You?'

Then He will answer them, 'Truly I say to you, to the extent that you did not do it to one of the least of these, you did not do it to Me.'

These will go away into eonian punishment, but the righteous into eonian life. (Matthew 25:31-46)

To those ridiculed and abandoned, I tell you the truth, that it was I, the Lord, who was ridiculed and abandoned.

Come to Me, all of you who are struggling and burdened, and I will give you rest. Take My yoke upon you and learn from Me, because I am gentle and humble in heart, and you will find rest for your souls. For My yoke is easy, and My burden is light.

(Matthew 11:28-30)

≈≈≈≈≈≈

Soon after leaving the school, I began asking myself, "What fruits were produced?" It's a worthy question to ask, don't you agree?

What are the fruits of your experiences? Every detail is important, no matter how big or small. Whatever is worthy of praise, thank God for it. For example, if it weren't for the quiet times and devotions at the school, I might have missed out on my unique, personal, intimate relationship with my Friend. If not for that relationship, I do not know how I would have survived the experience and its aftermath. The "hem of His garment" was just enough for me to hold on to; He was more real than anything I had experienced in my life before; and I refused to let go of that revelation.

Isaiah is one of my favorite books in the Bible. One afternoon, while crying out to God for His help, I came across the following chapter in Isaiah. As I read the words, I felt the chains that once held me down begin to break. Through these scriptures, and others, God has shown me what He was accomplishing during my time at the school, and long afterward.

> *Awake! Awake, Zion! Clothe yourself with your strength! Dress in your splendid garments, Jerusalem, the holy city! For the uncircumcised and the unclean will enter you no more. Shake off the dust! Arise! Be enthroned, Jerusalem! Loosen the chains on your neck, captive daughter of Zion!*
>
> *For thus says ADONAI: "You were sold for nothing, and you will be redeemed without money." For thus says Adonai ELOHIM: "Long ago my people went down to*

Egypt to live there as aliens, and Ashur oppressed them for no reason. So now, what should I do here,” asks ADONAI, “since my people were carried off for nothing? Their oppressors are howling,” says ADONAI, “and my name is always being insulted, daily. Therefore my people will know My name; therefore on that day they will know that I, the one speaking − here I am!”

How beautiful on the mountains are the feet of him who brings good news, proclaiming shalom [peace], bringing good news of good things, announcing salvation and saying to Zion, “Your God is King!” Listen!

Your watchmen are raising their voices, shouting for joy together. For they will see, before their own eyes, ADONAI returning to Zion. Break out into joy! Sing together, you ruins of Jerusalem! For ADONAI has comforted His people, He has redeemed Jerusalem! ADONAI has bared His holy arm in the sight of every nation, and all the ends of the earth will see the salvation of our God.

Leave! Leave! Get out of there! Don’t touch anything unclean! Get out from inside it, and be clean, you who carry ADONAI’s temple equipment. You need not leave in haste, you do not have to flee; for ADONAI will go ahead of you, and the God of Israel will also be behind you.

*"See how my servant will succeed! He will be raised
up, exalted, highly honored! Just as many were appalled
at him, because he was so disfigured that he didn't even
seem human and simply no longer looked like a man, so
now he will startle many nations; because of him, kings
will be speechless. For they will see what they had not
been told, they will ponder things they had never heard."*

(Isaiah 52, from the Complete Jewish Bible)

≈≈≈≈≈≈

Before I met Barbara, I trusted no one. I feared that
the turmoil happening inside me would be exposed. I had
worked hard to build a good name, and to restore my life
and my health. I did not want anyone to know I felt like a
failure. I refused to let the enemy steal yet another piece
of myself and I refused to give up those horrific years at
the school as wasted and worthless. My desperation
overruled my paranoia, and kept me from running away
many times while I was at the school. I was desperate for
truth. I knew it was "out there." I didn't know where it
was, or how to get it, but I knew it was out there
somewhere.

Does the desperation in your heart override your
torment—or your tormentors—today? Where do you go

from here? With whom can you talk? In whom can you
confide? Who can you trust?

I had nothing to lose when I met Barbara. As a
"lifestylist" today, I can tell you that anything you may be
protecting or defending will cost you more than you
would want to pay.

Are you ready to let it all go? Your answer to that
question will be the truest test of your heart. If you aren't
ready, how can anyone help you?

≈≈≈≈≈≈

I thank God for every day at the private school
program; I am grateful for all that He has brought me
through. Today, others are going through, coming out of,
or dealing with the aftermath of experiences similar to
mine. Who will share the *true* love of Jesus with them?
Who will say, as Corrie ten Boom declared triumphantly,
"There is no pit too deep that He is not deeper still."
Who will testify with the authority of having conquered
experiences like theirs, "Yes, you *can* have a victorious
life, no matter what you've been through...and here's
how!"

In the midst of whatever you may be going through
today, God knows, and He's there with you...waiting for

you to turn to Him. I pray that right now, you feel the strength of His arms wrapping around you. I pray that God surrounds you with flaming swords, protecting you from harm; that He close the doors that no longer serve His purposes in your life and open those that do.

> *And to the angel of the church in Philadelphia write: He who is holy, who is true, who has the key of David, who opens and no one will shut, and who shuts and no one opens, says this:*
>
> *"I know your deeds Behold, I have put before you an open door which no one can shut, because you have a little power, and have kept My word, and have not denied My name."* (Revelation 3:7-8)

A word of caution here: when the Lord begins to shut doors and open others, keep your hands off the doorknobs. He knows what He's doing!

> Lord, I pray that the love You have bestowed upon me, You will bestow on the reader of this book. Set each one free, oh, God!
>
> I pray, in Yeshua's mighty name, that the chains that once held you captive be broken off and fall away, once and for all, AMEN.

I pray that you would know just how real He is, right now, even if you have never felt His presence or His love before. God knows *who* you are and exactly *where* you are right now. You may not know it yet, but He's crazy about you!

You may wonder why He has allowed all the things that you have gone through—or are going through. I have asked myself that question too, more times than I can count.

I've seen many faces of hopelessness and despair, looking back at me from the past. I have to ask myself, "Who will help them?"

I understand pain!

I understand hopelessness!

I understand condemnation and guilt!

I understand LOST!

I also know a Friend who understands much more than I. He brought me through victoriously. His name is JESUS!

And Oh, how He loves YOU!

"Memories are the key not to the past, but to the future."

Corrie ten Boom

16

Five Steps to Victory

Some people say, "Don't sweat the small stuff," but I believe the "small stuff" keeps us bound. It's tedious to deal with because it's, well, SMALL. What if the small stuff is *exactly* what God is watching? Suddenly it isn't small anymore.

The steps that follow have helped me overcome obstacles and walk in freedom daily. They take time to master, but with consistent application, what took me a decade to learn will produce rapid results for you as you apply the principles and take action on your own behalf.

Some words of advice and encouragement first:

Take small steps. Some wounds heal faster than others, and life continues throughout the process. Take care of you. If God wants you to leap forward, He will provide sufficient grace. You are the only *You* we have, so be kind to yourself during this healing process!

Part of the healing process is an exercise in ruthless self love; loving yourself as God loves you. "Agape" love is of such high purpose that it was silent as God's own Son was beaten, ridiculed, and killed as a criminal to save you and me, who have done nothing deserving of such love. Agape is the greatest love that wins you to the Father. It doesn't always feel good, but *does* always accomplish His highest purpose for your life when you simply say "Yes" to Him.

Step 1: **Clean house on your insides.**

CLUTTER, CLUTTER, CLUTTER, GOTTA GO!

Emotional trauma often leaves our minds so "beaten" that we do not recognize what we are allowing into our spirits. We are the gatekeepers and no one else has access unless we open the gate. Evaluate what you have allowed and are allowing in your life that may not be God's highest and best.

What are you reading, watching, or listening to? These are three of the greatest influences on our subconscious minds. I realized, early in my recovery, that what I watched on television could take years to forget. I had to begin guarding my mind through the gates of my eyes and ears. I started looking for the purpose of what I read, watched, or listened to—a television show, music on the way to work, and even conversations going on around me. If there was no real, constructive purpose, I cancelled the distraction or I removed myself!

All of this took time; some distractions took years to clear out of the way. Why? Because I had to become sick and tired of being robbed of my time, awareness, and communion with God before I could release the distraction decisively.

Your healing is all about you and no one else. God is a "gentleman"; He will not *make* you do anything. He will ask you the same question Jesus asked the crippled man waiting by the pool of Bethesda: *"Do you wish to get well?"* (John 5:6). An old cliché says, "Some get bitter and some get better." Some get bitter and stop. YOU'RE STILL GOING, SO DON'T STOP! You have to be healthy enough to look that "thing" in the face—whatever has bound you—and say, "NO LONGER WILL YOU STEAL FROM ME AND MY LIFE!"

Ask yourself what you are allowing in your life that distracts or delays you from healing. The Word of God (the scriptures) keeps me focused, and has throughout my journey, even when I lived in a world that made little sense. Even if for only a few minutes a day, whether I felt it or not, spending time in the Word kept me connected to God.

I encourage you to keep pressing forward to victory. Your journey is the training that qualifies you for the calling of God on your life!

Step 2: **Clean your house. Yes, I said, *your* house!**

Clean and organize your home, car, and work space. I discovered that clearer thinking is built on a platform of order. Even if you are very organized already, look around you; whatever causes clutter and confusion in your life needs to GO! This step includes looking at people and situations in your life. Whoever and whatever is not healthy and holds you back—and you *know* who and what they are (family, friends, colleagues, significant others, jobs)—deal with it!

Change your location or change how you perceive your location. If you can't leave where you are, *receive* it— knowingly and deliberately—and learn from it with gratitude.

Step 3: **Find someone you can trust!**

I know this may be hard; it was for me. Ask God to show you whom you can trust and He will! My world was getting very dark until God put Barbara in my life. You need to feel safe. You need someone to be objective and who sees clearly, because much of what you have believed to be true may still be deceiving you. As you clear out the clutter and confusion, you need someone to stand with you, encouraging you to keep fighting for your freedom.

This is your life. Defend it steadfastly. Jesus bought you with His life so that you could live victoriously. I would love to wrap my arms around you and tell you that it's going to be okay.

Step 4: **Find a dream bigger than your pain.**

Many times our cluttered minds slow our forward progress. We can't think beyond tomorrow, or even beyond the next minute; just driving to work and dealing with the day may feel overwhelming.

What is your dream?

The scripture says, *"Where there is no vision, the people perish,"* (Proverbs 29:18). Without Vision—dreams and goals—we might rather die than wake up tomorrow. In the absence of vision, we don't participate in forming our life; yet it *will* take shape, but without vision, it may not be the shape we want, let alone be the highest and best that God has in store for us.

Let me give you a personal example of how a clear vision can empower your life:

As a child, I wanted to go to Africa. Whether it was to photograph or work with wildlife, or as a missionary, I didn't care; I just wanted to be there. I dreamt about what I would do and who I would help. I even got a book to learn Swahili because I imagined myself living in a small village in the Congo, where Swahili was the language. That dream kept me alive through many difficult times. God allowed that dream to be realized when I stepped onto the ground in Nigeria a few years ago. God truly blessed me by allowing me to see the great need of the people there. I saw that their hunger for Him far outweighed their hunger for food. It was a world apart from my own, literally and figuratively.

In the U.S. today, I am privileged to help meet needs and heal hurts of women who have survived emotional trauma. Many have had experiences similar to mine.

My own experiences have been completely worthwhile because of the joy of reaching someone and lifting her out of a pit of hopelessness and despair into the bright sunshine of victory. Perhaps the next person is YOU!

This is not about trying to forget about what you have been through, but about going beyond your circumstances, your pain and devastation. I did whatever I could during my search for healing. Of course I went about it all wrong! For example, I turned to alcohol in an attempt to blot out the suffering I still felt. Honestly, I *loved* drinking; I *loved* the places I went and the people I surrounded myself with to help me forget my pain. At the same time, I knew I was keeping God's highest and best and ultimately God Himself away from me. It broke my heart to recognize this about myself, because I knew that Jesus *already* knew!

I did not allow the Lord to heal me in *His* way UNTIL I became desperate to be free of the "killer" of my soul. I began to cry out to Him, "Please, Lord, remove this from my heart! I know You know I love it, but I don't *want* to love it, I want You MORE. Please make me hate everything about these self-destructive patterns!"

Step 5: **Stop blaming and forgive.**

This is pivotal to your healing: Blaming wastes lives, imparts no understanding, gives no comfort, offers nothing to the world, and leaves a person miserable. I have witnessed it many times since I began helping others recover from emotional trauma. Like a forest fire raging out of control, blaming rapidly consumes the life God gave you and leaves nothing behind but scorched earth.

People who may have hurt you, if they are alive, are most likely not thinking about you. Why waste another second pondering and reliving events or nursing feelings of bitterness or resentment when you need healing? I believe we all must go through a process of mourning painful experiences, but mourning must end; otherwise, God cannot rebuild your life!

Forgiveness is the key to unlock and stop the self-destructive and dead-end cycle of blaming. Forgiveness frees you to heal fully. *It's all about you!*

> *For if you forgive people their trespasses [their reckless and willful sins, leaving them, letting them go, and giving up resentment], your heavenly Father will also forgive you.*
> (Matthew 6: 14)

If I had continued blaming the people at the ministry center, I would have learned nothing from the experience. The journey would have been worthless and I would be unable to help anyone else today.

> *For you created my inmost being;*
> *you knit me together in my mother's womb.*
> *I praise you because I am fearfully and wonderfully made; your works are wonderful, I know that full well.*
> *My frame was not hidden from you when I was made in the secret place.*

When I was woven together in the depths of the earth,
your eyes saw my unformed body.
All the days ordained for me were written in your
book before one of them came to be. (Psalm 139:13-16)

I decided to declare my experiences worthwhile; not only for my sake or yours, but for Jesus' sake, because of the price He paid to make us whole! If anyone has a right to blame, it is Jesus, because people like you and me beat Him, ridiculed and killed Him!

If we declare our experiences to have been worthless—as if they should have been different, or should not have happened at all—we may as well declare Jesus' sacrifice equally worthless and a mistake; and that is obviously false!

Jesus said, *"The Son of Man did not come to be served, but to serve, and to give his life as a ransom for many"* (Matthew 20:28). He came to give his life—He came to die—and his death resulted in salvation for others. His blood was poured out for others. It was all for us!

...for this is My blood of the covenant, which is
poured out for many for forgiveness of sins.

(Matthew 26:28)

I recommend that you read the entire chapter of Isaiah 53, especially verse 5, which sums it all up:

> *But He was pierced through for our transgressions,*
> *He was crushed for our iniquities;*
> *The chastening for our well-being fell upon Him,*
> *And by His scourging we are healed.*

What are you doing that keeps you from victory? In helping young women recover from emotional trauma, I often find they forget that God created them and that He knows *everything*, from their weakest and most shameful areas to their greatest strengths and highest qualities.

I was desperate! I had to allow myself to get *brutally* honest about my frailties and sins before the Lord, because He already knew them. For a long time, I pretended that everything was perfect; that was how I survived. Ultimately, the burden was too heavy to bear.

If I may offer one more word of counsel, it is this: be BRUTALLY honest before the Lord. He hears you, and He has given this marvelous promise:

> *...for He Himself has said, "I WILL NEVER DESERT YOU, NOR WILL I EVER FORSAKE YOU..."* (Hebrews 13:5)

Today is all you have, so shake the dust off your feet and step into your life and watch your future, designed by your Father in heaven, unfold before you. It will all be worth it...I promise!

Are you ready to take your next step toward healing? Contact me for a free, no-strings-attached consultation:

Taylor@Taylor-Faith.com
www.Taylor-Faith.com

About the Author:

Taylor Faith's journey has taken her from being voted as one of the top hairstylists in the Washington, D.C. area to becoming a Lifestylist™. She combines her image-making skills with her experience in recovering from the ravages of emotional trauma. Her unique perspectives and keen sensitivities empower young women and lift them out of despair into victory.

Today, Taylor Faith specializes in helping women look, feel, and become the beautiful creations that God intended them to be.

Write to Taylor Faith:
Taylor@Taylor-Faith.com

Learn more about Lifestyling™ with Taylor Faith:
www.Taylor-Faith.com

www.ingramcontent.com/pod-product-compliance
Lightning Source LLC
Chambersburg PA
CBHW071437090426
42737CB00011B/1689